MW00476073

Lost in the Pacific

Epic Firsthand Accounts of
WWII Survival Against
Impossible Odds

Edited & Foreword by
L. Douglas Keeney

Published by Premiere

Published by Premiere
307 Orchard City Drive
Suite 210
Campbell CA 95008 USA
info@fastpencil.com
(408) 540-7571
(408) 540-7572 (Fax)
http://premiere.fastpencil.com

Edited & Foreword by L. Douglas Keeney

All Photos Courtesy: Author's Collection/Courtesy: National Archives

Maps Courtesy: CIA or University of Texas, Perry-Castañeda LibraryMap Collection,
as cited

Stories: United States Air Force Historical Research Agency, Maxwell Air Force Base,
Alabama

Manufactured in the United States by Courier Corporation
33120401 2014

First Edition

CONTENTS

FOREWORD: WHY LOST?

It was a beautiful day, everyone agreed. Sunny and warm but not humid, an unexpected break from the oppressive heat that usually blankets the South this time of the year. I was in Prattville, Alabama. I had decided to go to the Air Force History Center at Maxwell Air Force Base in Montgomery, Alabama, which was just two off-ramps down from where I had stopped for the night. I was researching a book on the history of air-sea rescue during World War II, and although my focus was on the technical aspects of it— the specialized types of seaplanes they used, the systems used to triangulate radio signals to find pilots, and so on—in truth, I had no idea what I was getting into.

I left at the crack of dawn and drove down to Montgomery and into the air base, but I found the parking lot full—the Italian Air Force had sent its pilots over for some joint training, I learned, and the building they used shared the parking lot I used. Nonetheless, I eventually got to the research room, where a dozen writing tables were surrounded by walls lined with filing cabinets filled with thousands of reels of microfilm. It was a lot of material, I supposed, but I knew it was just a fraction of the holdings locked beyond view in the vast three-story building beyond the secured doors.

I got to work. I had records pulled and thumbed my way through reports and folders that had been filed away untouched for 70 years. I looked at air rescue reports from the Atlantic theater and then the Pacific and, in time, I decided to focus on the Pacific theater exclusively. I was glad I did. I switched to the microfilm and whirred through crash reports and started to copy pages. *Thump;* the machine spit out a page, then another. I whirred through a new reel and saw another report and hit the print button. *Thump,*

thump, thump went the copier. I called for more paper, switched machines, and set up a second copier and punched out another report and then another. Some had titles—"Eleven Days in a One Man Raft", "Footsteps on the Beach", "Mission of VB-7"; others were just typed pages with a name, a unit, and a date. I hit the print button again and again; the stack grew.

World War II arrived at a time when airplanes were scarcely 30 years old. Engines were small, passenger capacity was limited, and only the largest of the flying boats had the fuel tanks and safety features necessary to cross the oceans. But war changed that quickly; and within a year, bombers and fighters were routinely crossing the Mediterranean, the English Channel, and—most daunting of all—the Atlantic and Pacific Oceans.

Piloting these aircraft were young aviators fresh out of pilot training, each the age of the average college graduate, 21 or 22 years old. They all had good reflexes and eyesight and were smart and healthy. They loved to fly and knew their planes inside and out; and they came to the Pacific eager to hunt Japs and end the war. They learned the new geography and the unfamiliar names of the countless islands they flew over—Guadalcanal, the Solomons, Choiseul, Layella Island, Samar, Negros, Iwo Jima. They knew the important choke points, the straits, where the Japanese air and naval bases were. They saw bullets, anti-aircraft fire, dogfights, and planes going down, many of them carrying their friends. They were young, but not frivolous. They were battle-hardened, but not without soft spots in their hearts for home. And they were scared, without losing their courage.

Naturally, the odds caught up with some of them. Engine problems, flak, dogfights, fuel leaks—and the planes crashed, ditched, landed on some spit of sand somewhere. They had survival gear, life rafts, "Mae West" life vests and dyes, mirrors, and even morphine, but the gear was only good for so much. The trick was to survive, and that took wits, too. The minute a plane ditched, a clock started ticking and it ticked fast. A man in the ocean without a life raft had maybe a day to survive, perhaps two. If he had a life raft, he could stretch it to 20 or 30 days, but that of course assumed he found water. The point is, the more ingenious and resourceful a pilot could be on his own, the better his chances were of survival. One pilot spent 20 days at sea, alone and adrift in a small raft, and survived by eating the partially digested fish he cut out of the stomach of an albatross. Another made it to land only to realize his island was an uninhabitable maze of endless snake-infested streams choked by vines and flowing into swamps, and surrounded by razor-sharp coral. He shoved off and drifted another two days until he washed up on an island with coconuts and water. One pilot landed on an island and was picked up by native guerrillas, who escorted him through a week of jungles before asking him to help them blow up a Japanese bridge. Another narrowly escaped the attack of an alligator; another was nearly eaten by what turned out to be an iguana on his chest; one had to help cut an airstrip out of the jungle so he could be evacuated; one survived alone at night bobbing in the ocean with only his head above the water.

Determination.

And an undaunted sense of duty. When they got back to their units, most of them had one request: to get back into the air.

Although this book is set in World War II, it's not a World War II book per se; but of course the war permeates everything. The battles are spread across the Pacific and pilots are flying missions against Japanese installations on dozens of islands, some of which you will know, but most of which will require a map. Half of the stories are of pilots who were bombing Japanese shipping or airfields or factories, and half are of pilots flying fighter planes to cover them. But all of them went through a lot. If they survived the blunt-force impact with the sea, they immediately faced a hail of bullets from the Japanese airplanes above or death from the sharks in the waters below. If they survived that, they faced days of unrelenting sun exposure and intense heat. And if that didn't get them, some had to survive ocean storms with towering, wind-driven waves that could flick them off into eternity as if they were mere gnats. And when they made land, every move on every island was taken with caution. The Japanese were watching everything.

There were more than 2,500 combat crash-and-rescue reports in the Air Force's History Center in Maxwell—maybe twice that. Most of them were little more than forms filled out by pilots at the end of a rescue; but for every 50 or 100 of them, there was an occasional first-person narrative, and of those, three or four had extensive detail. After three days of going through hundreds of reels of microfilm, I had more than 300 pages of first-person accounts, which I edited down to this book. I decided to add photographs, although that was a risky decision. There were no combat camera crews on the scenes, but as I researched various archives I found enough photos to show you where these men crashed, the airfields and aircraft carriers that were their homes, their survival gear, the planes they flew in, and, in many cases, the circumstances of their ordeal. No picture, though, is an exact match.

Each account is a testament to human resilience, character, fortitude. "All day long it was cold and rough," wrote one pilot of his fourteenth day alone in the middle of the ocean. "An albatross came and sat on the edge of the boat for about four hours. I stroked his neck and talked to himand he pecked my hand. He was Oscar, my friend."

They survived because they were smart, quick on their feet, and sometimes lucky, but always determined to live. They improvised with what they had, made do with what they could capture or kill, and suffered terribly. Pray your sons never have to go through this.

The publication of any book is occasioned by the opportunity to thank those who helped along the way, and I wish to do that now. I received invaluable assistance from the archivists at the United States Air Force Historical Research Agency located on Maxwell Air Force Base in Montgomery, Alabama, and to them I send my thanks. I could not have found these stories without the help of Lynn Gamma, Kevin Burge, and Leeander Morris, Jr.

Likewise, I wish to thank Vicki Whitmere, who transcribed the faded pages and made this book possible. I also wish to thank the half dozen readers I enlisted to read these stories and who urged me to have them published, foremost among them my wife, Jill Johnson Keeney, who edited great stories like these during her years as an editor for "New West"/California magazine.

I'd particularly like to thank Doug Grad of the Doug Grad Literary Agency, who helped me put these stories into a larger context, and Bruce Butterfield, my publisher at Premiere, who committed to this book after reading just 16 pages. Finally, thanks to my son, Alex Keeney, who is the talented writer in the family and who graciously accepted my invitation to pen his excellent history of air-sea rescue.

Creating and editing something like this allowed me to connect with a generation that I've struggled to connect with even though I have authored several of my own books on World War II. No longer. These are the distant voices of 25-year-olds, speaking their way, speaking as they would speak to a buddy in 1944, speaking to us today. To these young men, and to the thousands of nameless others who didn't make it home, I dedicate this book.

INTRODUCTION: AIR-SEA RESCUE IN WORLD WAR II

Alexander S. Keeney

In May of 1927, Charles Lindbergh became an international celebrity for completing the first transatlantic crossing by air, a 3,600-mile trip from New York to Paris in an airplane with a fuel tank where there should have been a windshield. So precious was the need for gas that Lindbergh would have to bank his plane to the side just to see what was in front of him.

By 1945, international air travel was routine—but it wasn't in small airplanes without a windshield, and it wasn't peaceful. By then, the airways over the Atlantic were thick with pilots ferrying bombers and fighters to England, while in the Pacific, formations of American B-29 Superfortresses were flying 20-hour missions round trip from Guam to hit the Japanese homeland; and over the English Channel and North Sea, B-17s and B-24s were bombing Germany in streams of eight and nine hundred planes each. As a matter of engineering, one generation's extraordinary had become the next generation's ordinary. Transoceanic flight was a way of life, but so too were its consequences. Into the oceans fighters and bombers fell, a single pilot bailing out of a burning fighter plane or an entire aircraft ditching belly-first into the churning seas. As these airplanes fell out of the sky, war planners were quick to realize they had a problem: how did they find and rescue these pilots and get them back alive?

The answers were not immediately evident even as the problem compounded. Yes, President Franklin Delano Roosevelt was correct when he boasted that "Hitler built a fortress around Europe, but he forgot to put a roof over it"; but suicide missions—missions with no hope of rescue if shot down over water—were hardly the kind of strategic power he was thinking of.

The early years of the war saw a long, painful process by which both sides learned through experience how to convert the tremendous potential energy of airpower into a kinetic force. It was high-stakes improvisation, where clashes with enemies and exposure to allies refined tactics and technologies. Aviation morphed from experimental to military, but the problems of air combat were more than matters of strategy and technology. The operational requirements of a two-front war meant that men and machines were constantly pushed to the limit. The requirements placed on aviation— plotted out from London to Moscow, and Hawaii to Tokyo—demanded that power be projected well past any existing safety net. The ocean that Charles Lindbergh had so narrowly crossed a generation before was now a superhighway in the sky and the first leg of any combat mission. The flight over water itself was not in question—fighter and bomber squadrons were equipped with aircraft that could make the trip—but when a plane crashed into the ocean, it was back to square one. Crews that survived a ditching, a slight miracle in and of itself, were drowning. Search and rescue had been an afterthought. Upon arriving in Great Britain in 1942, the United States Army Air Forces were wholly dependent on the British for rescues—and they themselves were struggling.

As early as 1935, Great Britain had established a token corps of marine rescue craft to monitor coastal waters for distressed aircraft and, when possible, provide rescue. This grew in subsequent years: British Air Command successfully developed high-speed boats tailored to search and rescue, inflatable dinghies were carried on board aircraft flying overwater routes, and a chain of command ending at reconnaissance units were created to provide forward control of the marine rescue.

But the outbreak of war proved this system obsolete upon implementation. Frustrated commanders quickly realized that SOS signals were lost in a decentralized chain of command that lacked adequate resources to provide meaningful assistance to pilots floating helplessly in the English Channel. The volume of downed air crews—one man per fighter, 10 to a bomber— overwhelmed the system.

As with many combat systems, trial and error informed progress; and in the grueling summer and fall of 1940, now recorded as the Battle of Britain, the importance of recovering lost aircrews transcended mere national security and verged upon national survival. Such were the stakes for air combat, whose victor would control the skies over the English Channel—and with it, the ability to invade the British homeland. Each RAF pilot was essential, and Britain's ability to recover them from friendly waters represented one of precious few advantages it had over the Nazi Luftwaffe.

Heavy combat in the air meant heavy losses and many more pilots ditching in the English Channel. The British consolidated air-sea rescue underneath a single command charged with coordinating air and marine assets to locate and retrieve the lost aircrews, as well as to develop new survival technologies for aviators to carry into battle. This consolidated command would equip pilots and their crews with survival necessities—life rafts, fresh water, rations, signaling mirrors, ocean dyes, flares, and emergency radios—as well as provide a multi-layered response mechanism for their safety and protection. Spotter planes were sent out to locate and circle downed pilots, re-purposed bombers and transports took off to drop supplies and lifeboats, and naval or coast guard ships were tasked to make the final rescue. It was a system that was refined, improved, and often improvised—and when technology was lacking, ingenuity blossomed. For example, spotter planes had to balance competing priorities: low-altitude flight was needed to maintain visual contacts with stragglers, but higher altitudes were needed to radio next-level rescuers. So rescue pilots learned to hunt in pairs: one to spot and one to radio.

In September of 1941 the net was widened. A full squadron of aircraft was authorized to perform "deep search operations"—rescues in waters greater than 20 miles from the British coast. The Royal Navy deployed to pre-established ditching stations as far forward as they could and wounded aircraft aimed to set down near one. Approximately one-third of all flyers lost at sea were now being rescued.

Much of the British success was, ironically, due to German innovation. As the U.S. Air Force's official history reads:

The RAF, and later the AAF, benefitted from observation of German equipment. The German rescue service perfected a one-man dinghy before

```
it was a feature of British fighter planes. They were the first to use
Fluorescine as a sea coloring to aid searchers in finding downed airmen,
and the first to discover that yellow was the best color for sea-rescue
equipment. In the fall of 1940 German sea rescue floats began to appear
in the English Channel. These had bunks for four men, blankets, food,
water and distress signals. The RAF copied the example.
```

It wasn't the last trick the British stole. Another Allied breakthrough came after capturing even more German technology in 1941, when British rescuers began finding downed German pilots floating in the English Channel with a personal radio transmitter. It was shaped like an hourglass so as to fit between their knees, waterproof, buoyant, and manually powered; and as the lost pilot hand-cranked its generator, it automatically transmitted an SOS signal on emergency frequencies. Radio signal direction finders homed in on these emergency transmitters and triangulated a solution. The German NS2 was genius and the Allies knew it. They copied and refined their captured product and the famous Gibson Girl emergency radio was born; and though American factories would produce this brilliant device, its application in the art of air-sea rescue was still strictly a British affair. British instructors, drawing on the hard-learned lessons of the early war years, would teach the Americans how to find and rescue their boys at sea. When Americans conducted their first successful integrated air-sea rescue mission on July 4, 1943, this investment paid its first dividend.

Unfortunately, no such network was available in the Pacific theater. Rather, the American forces had to build their own search and rescue capabilities from the ground up. Standardized distress procedures and SOS signal triangulation were useful for focusing search and rescue efforts in the English Channel, but the land masses were too far apart in the Pacific to make that possible, and new tactics had to be developed. And rare as it is in history, the U.S. Air Force attributes this effort to a single man: Major John H. Small, Jr., who arrived in New Guinea on December 11, 1942. Small was like his peers in that he sensed a need for an organized search and rescue corps in the Pacific; however, he was unlike his peers in that he elected to do something about it. With only a single enlisted man as an assistant, Major Small began directing search and rescue missions by any means available. Often, this included marshaling resources of the nearby Royal Australian Air Force. It also included begging for better equipment, like the OA-10, the

Air Force variant of the PBY Catalina flying boat. His efforts to organize local elements of the 5th Air Force into search and rescue teams drew the attention of neighboring commands, and by 1943, devoted search and rescue teams were stationed throughout the Southwest Pacific. They provided a layered response using spotter planes, large capacity transports or bombers to fly rescue dinghies and emergency supplies to downed pilots, surface ships, and, in increasingly large numbers, seaplanes and submarines.

But there were other problems. Unlike SAR in the European theater, where Great Britain and Occupied Europe represented fixed bodies of land and fixed front lines, the front in the Pacific was constantly on the move, sometimes shifting across hundreds of miles of ocean in the span of weeks. The dynamics of this expansive and changing front did not allow for the same network of fixed bases as the Atlantic. Rescue groups had to redeploy forward; others were often split up and scattered across the front.

Worse, the seas of the open Pacific were no place for the nimble, shore-based watercraft employed on the British coast, so American personnel learned to exploit technology more suited for the task. The Pacific theater thus became the showcase for "Flying Boats", or as lost pilots lovingly referred to them, "Dumbos", named after Walt Disney's flying elephant. The mainstay of the SAR air fleet consisted of the multi-engine PBY Catalinas and PBM Mariners, and the single engine OS2U Kingfishers. The Catalinas and Mariners launched from seaplane bases on land, while the Kingfishers were catapulted off ships or were also land-based. The workhorses, though, were the Catalinas. Their long over-water range, large interior cabins—including stoves, beds, and room for as many as two dozen or more survivors—and excellent observation blisters had already proven them to be fearsome submarine hunters; and their broad, aquatic hulls made them ideal for landings in the sea. A Catalina could drop down from the sky, make an open-water landing, pick up survivors, then ascend again to safety, or so the thinking went. But things were predictably more complicated, and there were tricks to be learned. Flying to and from calm coastal waters was one thing; taking off and landing in the high seas, hundreds of miles from shore, was another. Pontoons broke off, hulls cracked, and planes plowed into the waves and sank. In the end, it was usually life or death for the man in the life raft, so down the pilots went, balancing their throttles, timing the waves, skimming the surface until they had a place to let down. Throughout the war, time and again the pilots stretched their machines far beyond their design limitations to save just one more aircrew.

Surface ships also played a crucial role in Pacific air-sea rescue. When the bombers took off on long over-water missions, surface ships stationed themselves like highway markers across the ocean from airbases to targets. This gave damaged aircraft extra ditching stations to aim for and set down alongside. The fleet also sprang into action in the immediate aftermath of surface combat or invasions. After naval battles, ships and planes would come in to rescue downed pilots or crewmen from sunken ships bobbing in the oceans. In tighter spaces, closer to the enemy where aircraft and surface ships could not safely operate, appropriately-named lifeguard submarines would slink in just below the surface, emerge, and quickly pluck aviators from the top of the sea before retreating back below again. In some cases, airmen were too close to enemy shore installations for a conventional pickup. In those cases, smart-thinking sub captains simply extended their periscopes. The airmen would then toss a line around the periscope, like a modern-day hitching post, and be dragged out to sea, where the rescue could be completed without fear of Japanese fire.

Of course, pilots always made for land, but here they needed rescue too —and here they faced new perils. In most of the stories in this book, local natives were friendly toward Americans, but that was never a given. Avoiding capture was a mission that shadowed a survivor's every move. Sometimes friendly guerrillas were armed and organized, as was the case for pilots who fell into the hands of trained Filipino rebels or Australian coast-watchers, but coming ashore always meant returning to combat because vir-tually all of the inhabited islands in the Pacific were under the eye of the Japanese. It was jungle cloak and dagger.

Air-sea rescue only grew tougher as war in the Pacific War carried on. As the balance of air superiority tilted further in favor of the Allies, the skies became more and more crowded with American aircrews flying longer dis-tances to more disparate targets. Bombers and fighters were crashing every-where, often with full crews of 10 men. If they survived the impact, they faced the seas, sometimes drifting for weeks. Many perished while they waited. Some sank and were never seen again. Others became castaways and eventually died from exposure or starvation. The challenge of rescue was inseparable from the challenge of self-preservation. The basic C-1 survival vests, issued to all flight crew members, contained emergency equipment including sunglasses, hats, signaling mirrors, fishing kits, sewing kits, water bags, knives, 10 yards of bandages, matches, sea markers (fluorescents), compasses, signal whistles, first aid kits, rations, and signal flares. The survival vest was worn underneath a parachute and the Mae West life vest (so named because when the vest was inflated, the average male had a chest the size of actress Mae West's). For one-, two-, and three-seat planes, each crew member carried a personal dinghy attached to his parachute. It usually contained basic survival equipment like a sea anchor, bailing cup, first aid kit, repair kit, collapsible paddles, water, a sea marker, rations, distress signals, and a sail, and was inflated by pneumatic CO_2 cartridges that were pre-attached. Bombers came pre-loaded with large life rafts that contained survival provisions, including food, but as their missions outstretched the Dumbo's range, crews learned to take care of themselves, too. B-29s stuffed with emergency supplies often flew side by side with conventional bombers on strikes. When a plane ditched into the ocean, the rescue bomber fell out of formation with it, staying on site as long as fuel allowed. So desperate was the need for rescue facilities that planners could justify the Iwo Jima campaign on these grounds, to provide emergency facilities to wounded B-29s. But it still came down to surface ships, submarines, and Dumbos to pluck the men out of the water; and in the end, despite the daunting expanse of an enormous Pacific Ocean, Allied rescue efforts compared favorably to those experienced in the Atlantic theater. In the Pacific, approximately one-third of the airmen who survived a crash were rescued alive.

This book is, then, a story of survivors. It is easy to confuse survival with adventure, but to do so would be a mistake. There are fairy tale elements to each story: pilots shot out of the sky, surviving perilous landings and violent forces; airframes tearing apart in the swells; a raft in the storm, then lost at sea; adrift in paradise; washed up on a beach; secreted away by natives; nursed to life by some potion; and retrieved by submarines and flying boats to rejoin the fight. But to view this experience as an adventure is to ignore the truth of war. For every airman who was rescued, two were lost. For every man who was found alive on a floating raft, two died, blistered and dehydrated in the sun. Sharks swarmed. Enemies strafed. Cold water chilled. Bombers fell apart in the sea—half the crew reaching a raft, the other half sinking in the wreckage. In most cases, airplanes became flying coffins. And in many others, young men drifted in the ocean, hopelessly waiting for help that never came. There was no intelligence officer to interview the dead. Their stories were lost with them, swallowed in the sea.

This book is a monument to the courage of the aviators, rescuers, and natives who gave a second life to these young men; but it is dedicated to those who floated on the seas, never to be found and forever lost.

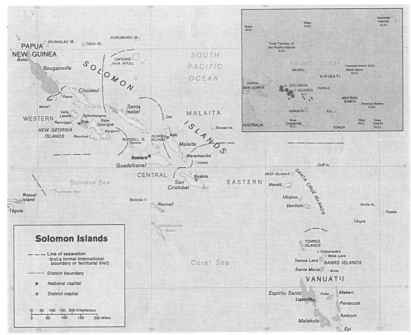

The Solomon Islands with Guadalcanal in the center. (Courtesy: University of Texas, Perry-Castañeda Library Map Collection)

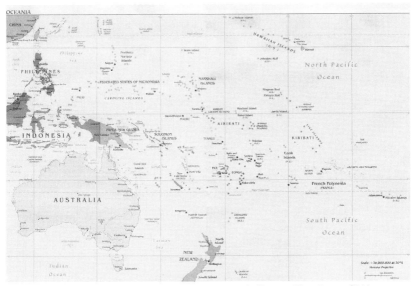

The South Pacific Ocean between Australia and China. (Courtesy: CIA)

1

32 DAYS

During the morning of 13 April 1943, Staff Sergeant W. I. Coffeen was one of 16 F4U pilots who took off to escort 12 TBF attack bombers on a bombing mission against Munda on New Georgia Island in the Southwest Pacific Ocean. Munda was an important target, a major Japanese supply base 150 miles north of Guadalcanal. Until Munda was neutralized, the American advance up the Solomon Islands was in jeopardy.

Coffeen was a Marine Corps fighter pilot. His job that morning was to protect the slower TBF dive bombers from attack while they bombed the Japanese base. He relates his experiences:

****

I was Major Peyton's wing man. We took off from Guadalcanal at 0530, rendezvoused with the TBFs according to plan and proceeded up the Northern coast of New Georgia and on reaching a point North of the mouth of Kula Gulf, at 12,000 feet, my engine began to fail, the propeller turning up 3,000 RPM, the oil pressure fell to zero and the engine began to smoke. I knew I was in serious trouble so I called to Major Peyton and told him I was returning to base. I did not talk over my radio again, because we were on radio silence and I was afraid of giving away the position of our striking force. I turned my plane around and started in the direction of my base, but my plane was losing altitude very fast and could only make 100 knots. I realized the plane was about to blow up and I could not possibly make it home, so when I was about 3,000 feet I climbed out of the cockpit and dove off into space. I was very low when I bailed out and my parachute opened just before I hit the water. The plane hit the water only a short distance from me. I had cut the switches off, so it did not explode, but sank immediately. My parachute leg straps were not tight so when the parachute opened, the sudden jerk caused my right leg strap to gouge into my right hip, resulting in a cut and bruise about 4 inches long. I did not notice the injury at the time because I had too many other thoughts to occupy my mind. The chute fell clear of me and I was able to free myself right away. I attempted to inflate my Mae West life jacket but there was a hole in it so it did me no good. I then released my rubber boat and after fooling around with it for a minute or two I succeeded in inflating it and climbing aboard. An instant after I had gotten into the boat I saw two fins sticking out of the water and heading directly for me. I figured they were sharks but could not see them very well, though they passed so close to my boat that I could have touched them with my hand. I did not take my backpack off until I got into the boat, so I salvaged all of its contents.

The sun was still shining and I could see Choiseul to my North and Kolomangara to my South. I was about equidistant from each. I took my backpack off and took out the contents to see what their condition was. The pack had leaked and everything in it was soaking wet, so I spread them out on my boat to dry in the sun. I could find no paddles, the water was calm, but I could see storm clouds gathering in the Southeast so I started paddling with the current, toward the Islands at the Southeastern tip of Choiseul Island, using my hands as paddles.

During the afternoon 4 P-38s and 4 F4Us passed over me at about 12,000 feet, heading North. My flares were wet and worthless, as were my matches, also my compass. I fired my pistol five times and waved the sail that I had in the boat, but to no avail. The planes apparently did not see me. I was a bit discouraged at this, but had hopes that they had seen me or would see me on their return. I continued to paddle toward the islands and about sundown the P-38s and F4Us returned, flying very low. Two F4Us passed within 500 yards from me, one on each side, and about 100 feet off the water. I fired my pistol, waved everything I had, shouted and did everything I could to attract their attention, but they in no way indicated that they had seen me. I had slight hopes that they had seen me and would send a Dumbo to pick me up.

Soon after the planes had passed the storm hit. Rain, wind, and waves tossed my boat in all directions. I was still attempting to paddle when finally a wave capsized my boat dumping everything I had into the sea, little of which I was able to recover. I had taken my shoes off, which was a fatal mistake, and they were lost. The four-ounce bottle of brandy was lost, but I did get one swig of it beforehand. I saved my poncho, sail, knife, mosquito head net and pistol. The pistol soon became worthless from rust so I threw it away along with 14 rounds of ammunition. The storm blew me through the slot below Wagina Island and out to sea, to the North, but I was not blown beyond the sight of land.

It got dark and the waves were high and I realized that paddling was useless, so I decided to make myself as comfortable as possible, conserve my energy and trust to the wind and currents until morning. The boat was too short and I couldn't stretch out full length, as a result of which, in addition to other discomforts, I did not sleep at all. The wound in my right side was by this time very painful and uncomfortable.

I was not particularly scared after I bailed out of my plane, that possibly frightening all future fright out of me. I did not have much faith in the rubber boat, expecting it to collapse any time, so my main aim was to get to land as soon as possible. There was no pump on the boat, just a little rubber hose that I blew into every time the boat needed air.

The next day, at sunrise, the water was calm and I was approximately three miles to the North of land. I paddled the entire day, until sundown; at which time I reached a small island South of Choiseul. The sun by this time had burned my face very badly, my lips were swollen and parched and my side was continuously aching, all of which made me most miserable, but I hadn't eaten since dawn the previous morning and was getting very hungry and thirsty. When I reached the island I went ashore and got two coconuts which I opened, drank the juice and ate the meat. This satisfied my appetite and thirst a good deal and I felt a bit more comfortable.

I decided to make this island my home for the night and just as I had pulled my boat up on the shore and finished camouflaging it with foliage, a Jap float Zero passed over my head but, thank heavens, he did not see me. The mosquitoes were terrific and I didn't like the idea of sleeping on the bare ground with all the insects, land crabs, etc. crawling around, so I used the boat for a bed. I wrapped my feet in the sail, soaked my undershirt and put it over my head, tucking the ends down into my dungarees, then put my mosquito head net over the top of the undershirt. I slept on my back, my arms folded, hands tucked into my dungarees and covered completely by my poncho. As tired as I was I slept very little. The mosquitoes buzzed around like a flight of four engine bombers. I remained on this island about two days, trying to get my bearings and all the time hoping that someone would see me. I circled the island, trying to find some signs of life, but it was all swamp land. To the south of me I could see what appeared to be a large island and what I imagined to be Santa Isabel, so I made up my mind I would try to get there the next day. I started out early the next morning, still using my hands as paddles, for fear that a wooden paddle might puncture my boat and by now I fully appreciated the value of the boat under these circumstances. I reached this island about sundown and soon realized that it wasn't Santa Isabel. Later it was identified as Wagina Island.

After spending the night on this island in the same manner that I have already described, I began the next day an exploratory examination of the island. There was quite a lot of wild life such as wild pigs, some of which were quite large, pigeons, wild chickens, etc. Though I didn't go into the question too thoroughly, the pigs apparently were not vicious and dangerous, but were timid and fled at the sight of me. I thought, with this wild life, there would be some people on the island, but it was uninhabited.

The next morning I felt fairly strong. I decided that I couldn't profit by remaining on this island any longer so I started in a northwesterly direction (toward Choiseul). I at least couldn't land in any worse spot. I continued in this direction for the next few days, sleeping at nights on small islands, one of which apparently had been inhabited, because I saw writing on the rocks and trees, but found no people.

One night while sleeping on the beach I had my poncho spread over my body, when I heard something walking toward me that sounded a good deal like a man. I felt this body crawl up on my chest. It scared me so I pushed the poncho up, throwing the object off of me, grabbed my poncho, jumped into my boat and pushed off from shore. On looking back I saw what is called an "Iguana." It was a terrible looking monster that had bowed front legs similar to an English Bulldog, the shape of a lizard only very large, about four feet long. It was standing on the beach, ready to strike like a snake, his tongue spitting out at me. To my relief he did not attempt to follow me.

The rats were plentiful and were all sizes, from the size of a large mouse to that of a rabbit. Nearly every night they would play all around me and often wake me up by running across my body. On a number of occasions I was awakened by rats nibbling at my fingers, but, thank goodness, these were the smaller type.

About the 7th or 8th day after I had bailed out, I was in my boat attempting to open a coconut with my knife, when all of a sudden the knife slipped and cut a hole in the bottom of my boat. (A very foolish oversight.) The boat started deflating, so I got my sock and jammed it into the hole, making only a slow leak. At intervals I would have to inflate the boat. From this time on I had to keep my foot over the hole all the time I was in the boat.

Having no shoes was a terrific handicap. It was hard enough to walk along the shores of the coral islands at first when my feet were o.k., but soon my feet received many cuts, which turned to infections and I could hardly walk at all.

I traveled like this for days, all the time living off coconuts. I passed through Manning Strait and reached Taore Peak, on the southeast corner of Choiseul. There were many small coconut islands all around this section, but there were no coconuts here. A storm came up so I lived under a ledge in the side of the hill, staying here 5 days, and eating nothing. I didn't know what the native fruits or foods looked like. There were pigs and wild life here, but I could catch none of them.

I left this spot and retraced my path. The storm was still going on and the water was rough, but I managed to make it fromisl and to island, where I found coconuts. I had been gone about 15 days and was getting very depressed. I finally ended up at a coconut island which I think the plantation owners called Big Island off the southwest point of Choiseul. There was

a house on a small island to the South and, after 3 days on Big Island, I
decided to go and investigate the house on the smaller island, so at sun-up I
started for this small island, reaching there about noon. At this time I was
suffering from diarrhea, and lost a lot of weight and was breaking out all
over my body with sores which were infected, contained puss and itched a
great deal. The glare of the sun had given me a very painful headache that I
carried with me the whole time. I was very weak and was near giving up.
This was about the 20th day.

I spent the night on the beach and the next morning I started for the
house, approaching it very cautiously, for fear that it be occupied by the
Japs, but no one was there. My teeth were getting loose, hurting quite a lot,
my gums were terribly sore and chewing anything would have been impossible. I went through the house but saw no signs of life. The Japs had been
there though. On the front of the house was a sign, "Solomon Developing
Co.", Salincea Estate, located 7th and Bridge Street, Sydney, Australia. I will
never forget the name and if I ever get to Sydney I am going in to see the
man and thank him for his hospitality. I found some limes, which I squeezed
in some water in a coconut shell, and drank it. I was thinking how nice this
limeade would be with a little ice and a tall tumbler. I found an old hen in a
small chicken house in the back of the main house. When I saw this hen I
thought "Oh Boy! What a stew I'm going to have now!" The old hen had a
sort of dead look in her eye so I was afraid she might be sick and might
poison me. I poked her with a stick and she jumped up and ran away,
showing plenty of life. A terrific chase ensued but I was unable to catch her.
However, she left a full dozen eggs in her nest. I cracked one of them and
smelled it and it was obviously rotten, but I was so hungry that I couldn't let
a little matter of this kind interfere, so I threw the egg down my throat and
chased it down with water. I ate the full dozen, eating two a day. I did not
suffer any ill effects from those eggs. I stayed at this house for three days.
When I left I took some limes and the remainder of the eggs with me. While
here my hand became infected so I cut it with my knife to make it bleed and
then kept it in the rays of the sun which eventually healed it up.

I decided to try and make it back to the island I landed on first (Wagina),
but the current was so strong and I was growing so weak that I saw I
couldn't make it, so I returned to the island on which the house was located.

On reaching the beach I struggled up the hill to the house, so weak I could hardly make it, and spent the night at the house sleeping very soundly. The next morning my shoulders were so stiff and painful that I could hardly move my arms. My hands by this time were infected and a mass of sores from paddling in the salt water. I stayed at the house for three or four days to try and regain my strength. I could hear the chicken in the bush and once in a while she came within view but I was too weak and weary to try and catch her. I ate only coconuts.

On leaving the island I started NW along the coast and what I thought was the mainland, but turned out to be a number of little islands and lagoons. The sun was terrific and my face was terribly burned. My lips were so bad that they would bleed when touched. My eyes were swollen and gave off matter so that I would have to break them open in the morning. I had pains in my right side that doubled me over a number of times. I did not know what was wrong, but thought maybe it was from gas in my stomach. This night I slept on Rob Roy Island which I thought was the mainland of Choiseul. The next morning I went inland, found fresh water and wild life but no signs of people, so about noon I decided to start up the coast again.

During all this time I saw quite a few Jap float planes, but don't think any of them saw me. On one occasion I was right out in the open when a float plane flew directly overhead. I thought maybe he would take a shot at me, and didn't give a damn whether he did or not, but apparently he must not have seen me.

I finally came to an opening in these islands at a point where I could see Taore Peak, where I had been about 15 days before, so I started to head through a passage, in that direction, but a storm caught me and blew me down along the SW coast of Choiseul. I pulled my boat ashore and dumped the water out, then got back into it and shoved off. I decided to try and get back to Taore Peak but another storm caught me and blew me back and out toward the channel. I tried to get ashore on a small island where I decided to get some rest, but before I got there I collapsed, through exhaustion.

I do not remember much about it, but when I had stopped to dump my boat I had become delirious, completely out of my head, screaming, raving and yelling at the top of my lungs. A native saw me and followed me in his boat until I collapsed. The next thing I knew he was along side of my boat and asked me if I was Jap or American. I called out "me American." He put me into his boat and I knew nothing else until I realized he was carrying me, in his arms, to his hut where he put me on a board bed. I was so weak that I couldn't walk. I could understand him fairly well. My ankles, legs and joints were swollen and I was so exhausted that I fell fast asleep. I had told him I was starved and the first thing I knew, his three little sons, Tikus, Amos and Fabus, turned up with yams, sugar cane, Pau Pau and some fish, called Pith. They awakened me and gave me some sugar cane from which I sucked the juice. He cooked the yams, fish and Pau Paus in a coconut shell, and squeezed the coconut shredding into it. It was the first hot food I had had to eat for 32 days, and it really tasted good. After this they put me to bed and the next day I felt only slightly better. He still had to carry me wherever I went. This being Saturday (Sunday to him, because he was a Seventh Day Adventist) he waited until the next day to take me to a native village called Boe Boe (a Methodist village). The native, his wife and four sons took me there in a boat. I stayed here three days and ate the same things until the third day when Lukeana brought me some Swift's corned beef with rice which I ate for one day, but got indigestion and couldn't eat anymore. They gave me big bowls of it and I felt that if I didn't eat it all they would feel hurt. (Lukeana was the name of the native that picked me up.)

The village had native huts all around in a coconut grove. They had gardens stuck back into the bush. Only a few native men stay in the villages, the others live back into the bush. They were very friendly and seemed to delight in shaking my hand, under the least provocation. They saw I was pretty sick and thought I had malaria, so they introduced me to "Queenie". "Queenie" is the name they use for Quinine. They also took me to see the healing falls, which frightened me a little, wondering whether they were going to give me some kind of initiation, but to my delight this is where I received my first fresh water bath. They used half of a lime as soap. I don't know what that did to my skin but it stung like the devil. The third day they brought the women down to see me. They all shook my hand and brought me shells, sugar cane and other trinkets.

It was very interesting to note the passages that the natives traveled through in their canoes. It would appear as though they were paddling straight into an island but on reaching the island they would part the bushes and there ahead would appear a nice channel, through which to pass.

We got permission from the District Chief (Zaro) to leave Boe Boe and proceed to his village at Pasarai, traveling by canoe, where we met Zaro about noon. I didn't know where I was at this time, but I had been told it was Choiseul. I didn't know the day of the month. Lukeana told me it was May 6 and I thought "My goodness! Have I been gone that long?" Then on reaching the next village a native missionary told me it was May 15th. We heard that there were two float planes down nearby, and word was sent to us not to proceed until the next day. The next day we traveled up to another village, arriving there just before night. During the night we heard four Jap barges along the coast. I had been here two days when a native who spoke good English came and stayed with us and kept me company for the next few days.

Giripuko, who was chief of the native police, scouted all the villages along the coast in search of the Japs. He located them in a village above us.

Lukeana, Publulu, Zaro, Gripuico, and two others rowed me to a village farther up the line where we slept that night. We traveled by night. We passed right by the village where the Japs were and could see their fires very palely. Later we learned that a barge of 150 Japs were camped within ½ mile from us. Pabulu must have had a sixth sense, because he wouldn't let us eat breakfast there and made us go into the bush to do our cooking. This was a lucky move.

They took me inland about 5 or 6 miles where I stayed for a month, was fed good food and regained part of my strength. I ate spam, Vienna sausage, yams, etc. During this time I had a very severe case of malaria, but got through it all right. I had gained 20 pounds before returning to Guadalcanal.

One day I was taking a bath in a river when a native called out "Look out, there's an alligator," and at the same time he fired a shot with a rifle. I scrambled up on the beach scared to death, but the native's shot was true. The alligator was coming right for me, but was stopped in his tracks.

One day they roasted a pig for me. They shaved the pig, leaving the skin on, and roasted it on rocks, around hot coals. They cut off slices which they gave to me to eat. It was very delicious and quite a treat.

Contact was finally made with Guadalcanal and a PBY was sent for me on June 25, and I was returned to Florida Island, where I was put in a hospital. I stayed there over night and was transferred to Guadalcanal the next day. My squadron was there on their second tour and I sure was glad to see them. I wanted to get in a plane and start right out again, but no soap.

The members of my squadron informed me of the fact that Major Britt was killed during the takeoff for the same flight that I was on when I was forced to bail out. I can understand what happened to him because the same thing almost happened to me. There is a red light in the top of the trees on the South side of the East end of the runway, another in the top of the trees on the North side and a third red light on top of the tower off the North side about 50 yards and halfway up the runway. He no doubt was in a hurry and lined up with the light at the northeast and the tower-light and proceeded to take off thinking he was lined on the two lights at the end of the runway. He most likely never realized his mistake until he crashed. I almost made the same mistake myself.

Epilogue

Coffeen survived a bailout, parachuted into the ocean, made it into his raft just as sharks appeared, spent endless days alone and adrift, and spent weeks alone on uninhabited jungle islands. He suffered from infections, boils, sunburn, delirium, and malaria. He barely avoided being killed by an alligator and evaded detection by the Japanese—and finally made it back to his base. For most people, that would have been enough, but like so many men of his day, he had only one wish: to get back into the fight.

What was his mission? Guadalcanal was the largest island in the strategically important Solomon Islands, a chain of Pacific islands that were directly in the path of ships and planes going to and from Australia. If the Japanese owned the Solomons and then took New Guinea, Australia would have been cut off completely. When news came in the summer of 1942 that the Japanese were building a larger air base there, Guadalcanal became a military priority and it was invaded in August of 1942 and freed in January of 1943. SSgt. Coffeen's squadron, F4U Corsairs of VMF-213, the Hellhawks of the United States Marine Corps, moved ashore, among the first to be based in the Pacific.

The pilots had breakfast at Henderson Field before liftoff at 5:30 AM. Coffeen's job was to escort a group of slower and more vulnerable TBF torpedo bombers. Unfortunately, his engine failed somewhere between Choiseul Island and Kolomangara Island off New Georgia. He bailed into the Pacific Ocean near the southern tip of Choiseul and spent the next four weeks paddling between the uninhabited islands located in that area. He was slightly off the beaten track, and because of that, fewer planes patrolled the area. In the course of almost a month, Coffeen moved not more than a few miles from where he had bailed out.

2

IT WAS A FRIENDLY, FULL MOON

Lieut. (jg) G. Smith, USNR

(Lieut. Smith kept a brief diary on a piece of rubber patching material, from which much of this story is taken.)

****

On July 14, my flight took off from Guadalcanal at 1330 for a routine combat patrol over Rendova and Munda. We were flying Grumman Wildcats. En route to Munda we encountered a series of thunderheads that were so well developed that we could neither go over nor under them. We were, however, able to circle the storm to the south and arrived on station an hour late.

Although our mission was combat patrol, we found it necessary to start home almost immediately, for we had barely enough gas to get us home by skirting the storm to the south as we had done coming in. We decided that it would be best to fly "on the water," following the coast of New Georgia as far as possible, then go "on instruments." Flying through the clouds on instruments, we hoped to break out by the time we got to the Russell Islands.

My compass unfortunately was not working, so my only hope was to fly wing on someone whose instruments were all intact. Shortly after entering the clouds at the eastern end of New Georgia, our formation dispersed and every man was on his own. It would have been foolish for me to continue on instruments with a compass I couldn't depend on, so I returned to Rendova. I decided to try to go around the storm to the south and possibly get close to the Russell Islands before running out of fuel and facing a landing in the water. I followed that plan, but the storm had moved farther south; and when I came down in the water at 1900, I was 50 to 70 miles south of the Russell Islands.

Landing a Wildcat on the ocean is like dropping a pebble on the water. The water impedes its progress, but it continues to go down. After the belly of my plane hit the water, the plane went forward 15 or 20 feet, then nosed down for Davy Jones' locker.

Fortunately, I was prepared. I had the hood locked open, and I had an extra canteen and an extra emergency kit on my parachute harness. My shoulder straps and safety belt were drawn as tight as I could get them. When the plane stopped its forward motion, I disengaged the safety harness, kept my parachute buckled on me, gave a hard push with my legs, and went about five feet up to the surface of the water.

My rubber raft was of the small, one-man, seat-pack type that is an integral part of the seat-type parachute. Once in the water, it took about five minutes to unpack and inflate the raft. It was dark when I landed on the water, but despite that fact I finally succeeded in removing and inflating the raft. I dumped my heavy, water-soaked parachute pack into the raft and painstakingly worked myself aboard, being careful all the while not to capsize the raft and run the risk of losing it in the dark. Completely exhausted, I lay athwartships for almost five minutes, vomiting up the sea water I had swallowed during the struggle in the water. When I was sufficiently rested, I worked myself farther into the raft and assumed the sitting position from which, but for a very few exceptions, I was not to stir for twenty days.

The night air blowing through my water-soaked clothes gave me a chill, but I shivered from nearly two hours before I finally weakened and decided to unpack my parachute to use as a blanket. Once unpacked, the chute was so big and clumsy that there was not room in the raft for all of it. I, therefore, cut off half the shroud lines and stowed them in the raft against possible future need and cut off the top half of the canopy to use as a blanket. The rest I tied in a bundle, secured it to the raft with an eight-inch length of shroud line, and, along with the pack and harness, threw it overboard.

By this time, the moon was well above the horizon. It was a friendly, full moon, which I was destined to observe through one complete phase before it finally disappeared to leave me lost and lonely during endless blank nights. I knew that ships no longer sailed the waters of the Coral Sea. Also, I knew that planes were not likely to be out there at night, so I decide to try to get a little sleep. Unable to lie down in the little raft, I devised a method of sleeping in the sitting position. I tucked my parachute silk under my feet, pulled it back over my knees and over my head, then tucked it in behind me. The silk would then support my head, throwing the weight against my feet. Even with that device I was unable to get more than two or three hours of sleep each night. The waves and swells were consistently ten to twenty feet high. As soon as I would doze off, a wave would break over the boat and wake me up; then I would bail out the water and doze again; another wave, and so on into the night.

The days were hot, the nights were cold, and the wind and waves were merciless. To combat the heat of the day I kept my flight suit, helmet, shoes, sunglasses, and even my gloves on. I made a mask out of parachute silk for my face. As a result I suffered very little from sunburn. My light brown hair bleached to a pale yellow despite the protection offered by my helmet.

The wind and waves presented a much more difficult problem than the sun. I kept my sea anchor out so the raft would ride "bow-into-the-waves." At night, my parachute silk reduced the shock of being hit by breaking waves, but it did not keep me dry. The constant pounding of the waves was nerve-wracking. I soon started cussing at them. The cussing gave way to screaming, and then I got hold of myself. I stopped and prayed for strength to withstand the merciless pounding.

I carried morphine syrettes in my emergency kit for relief from severe pain. When my nerves seemed near the breaking point, I used the morphine to give me relaxation. When I was under the influence of the dope, the pounding of the waves ceased to irritate me. I resorted to it on three different occasions, all of which were at night.

The three weeks that I spent adrift in the Coral Sea were not without their exciting moments. I had always wanted to see a whale, and during the first week that wish was fulfilled six times. The first appeared on July six-teenth. I heard a noise like large rollers breaking on a beach. Looking in the direction of the noise, I saw two whales of the sperm whale or blackfish type. One was coming right toward my raft. He would roll on the surface of the water, blow, then submerge for almost 100 feet before coming to the surface to roll and blow again. I tried to paddle out of his way but could make no headway in the heavy sea. I thought of shooting him with my pistol but soon realized that I could not kill him with such a small weapon and that the shot would just enrage him. I put my pistol and paddles away, checked to see that all my equipment was secured to the raft, inflated my "Mae West" and waited for the crisis. The whale came to the surface, put his nose against the starboard side of the raft, pushed it about ten feet through the water, then slid under the boat. He was about forty feet long and, as he slid under me, every inch of the forty feet seemed like a mile. The water was clear as a crystal ball, and I watched that huge mammal submerge on the port side of the raft. He continued on his way, rolling and blowing as he went.

At dusk on July eighteenth, I heard a very violent splashing off my port beam. On closer observation I saw what appeared to be a fight between a marlin and a mackerel. The marlin was seven or eight feel long, had an eighteen-inch "spike," and apparently was trying to catch the thirty-inch mackerel. The two fish came directly toward my raft, and the last time they jumped out of the water and splashed back in they were just three feet from me. I had visions of the marlin's "spike" piercing my raft and leaving me on the ocean with a seat. God must have been with me, for the fish disappeared and I didn't see them again.

On July twentieth, I saw the first of many Japanese planes that I was to see before being rescued. I drifted on course of 300 degrees deep into enemy waters. I saw an average of one plane a day from then on, some friendly, some enemy, and others too far away to be recognized. I signaled some with tracer ammunition from my .45, with a mirror which I flashed in the sun, and with sea marker dye. But not a one was to see my signals until August first.

On July twenty-fourth, I saw the first shark. Ordinarily, the sea anchor held the bow of the raft into the waves, but around 1330 on this day, I noticed that I was riding sideways up the waves. A fish line which I had secured near the center of the starboard side of the raft was taut and drawn out at a ninety degree angle to the side of the raft. Suddenly, the fish line snapped, the raft swung back to its usual position, and a shark's fin broke the surface of the water. He swam under the raft and with his dorsal fin cut a fish line that I had secured to the port side. Thinking a dead shark would float, I tried to shoot him. The bullet "struck home." The shark jumped from the water, then floundered and sank. The same thing happened when I tried to shoot a mackerel so I decided not to waste ammunition on fish.

On July twenty-eighth and twenty-ninth, half a dozen sharks were with me day and night. Only one, however, made an attempt to attack, and it was a small one about four feet long. Most of those that I saw were at least six or seven feet in length. My lone would-be attacker rolled over on its side and turned almost belly-up to get into position to bite. I could see its curved mouth, ugly teeth, and beady, pig-like eyes. But again God was with me. My enemy failed to carry through his attack.

At dusk on July twenty-ninth, a huge wave threw the raft end-over-end. Luckily, I had all of my equipment securely lashed to the raft, and the raft itself was secured to my body by a twelve-foot length of shroud line. I had seen sharks less than half an hour before, and now I thought of the possibility that they were still lurking unseen in the black water.

At one point in my training I had been told that sharks were cowards and that they would hesitate to attack a man that moved violently, so I kicked and splashed with all my might while I righted the raft. I succeeded in getting aboard with little difficulty and was happy to find that not a single article of equipment had been lost.

On August first at 0900, after seeing nothing but Japanese planes for several days, a New Zealand land-based Lockheed Hudson passed very close to me. The tail gunner saw the sea marker dye I had spread on the water.

The plane turned, made a wide circle, and flew down close to the raft. For the first time in my life, and I hope the last, I cried for joy. The New Zealander circled for about an hour. I was afraid they would check my position and leave without dropping supplies; and, frankly, I was getting pretty hungry and thirsty by this time. I put on my rubber paddles, leaned back in the raft, and signaled in semaphore the letters E-A-T. They made another wide circle and then dropped an inflated life jacket with supplies attached.

The bundle hit the water about thirty feet from my raft. I paddled to it and found Army-type emergency rations, a canteen of water, a map marking my position, ammunition for my .45, a water-proof flashlight, first-aid equipment, a Very pistol and star shells, and other useful items. I was hungry but ate sparingly, not knowing how soon I would be rescued. The New Zealanders flew by once more, wobbled their wings, and headed for home.

I watched for the rescue plane the rest of that morning and all that afternoon, but none appeared. I watched, waited, hoped, and prayed all day of August second, but there was no rescue in sight.

About 2300 on August second, my raft capsized again. As I was rather weak by this time, it took me about fifteen minutes to turn my raft over and get aboard. During the struggle I lost my parachute silk blanket and a pencil I had been using to keep a log. I was in misery the rest of the night. It was then that I realized how much warmth the parachute had provided.

August third was a dreary day. Mist and thunderstorms were all around me. I didn't expect rescue. I was convinced that I had drifted so far out of position that the rescue planes couldn't find me. I was, therefore, a surprised and happy man when, at 1100, I spotted three Navy Catalina flying boats approaching me. Two passed within half a mile, but failed to see me. The third passed directly overhead and saw the sea marker dye I had spread on the water.

He dropped a smoke bomb to mark my position, called the other planes back, and all three circled the raft. The waves and swells were ten feet high. It would have been a rough sea for any craft, let alone a flying boat.

Two of the planes lowered their retractable wing floats and made an attempt to land. Both pilots decided, upon closer observation of the waves, not to risk "setting down" on such a choppy sea. About that time I drifted into a rain squall and the rescue planes lost sight of me completely.

The third pilot, Lieut. (jg) Hamblin, was a little more venturesome than the other. Although he could not see me, he decided that if one of them did not land on the water in that vicinity, they would probably never find me again. He dropped his depth charges and about 900 gallons of gasoline (I'll bet that breaks your heart) to lighten the plane and made a power-stall landing on the water. His starboard wing float hit a swell as he was landing and started to spin the plane to that side. Hamblin proved to be the master of the situation. Quick as a cat, he hit the throttle on the starboard engine, and kicked the rudder and stick to port.

The lumbering Catalina straightened out and dropped into the sea. A wave broke over her and smashed the port gun blister and filled the after compartment with water. The plane remained afloat, however, and the crew bailed out the water as Hamblin taxied into the squall where I had disappeared. After taxiing about two miles, they found me, gorging myself on the last of the rations that had been dropped to me on August first.

Despite the Catalina's precarious position on a heavy sea in enemy waters, I for one was in the lap of luxury. I stretched out on a dry bunk, pulled a warm blanket over me, drank some fresh water, and smoked a cigarette while I waited for O. Braun, one of the crewmen, to fix me something to eat. Practically the entire crew was seasick, and Braun was no exception. Nevertheless, he fixed me two tumblers of grapefruit juice, a couple of cups of coffee, two big steaks, and a large dish of peas.

The sea was so rough that Hamblin decided not to risk a take-off at that time. He asked me if the water ever got any smoother out there, but I couldn't offer him much encouragement. Although the waves were running at least ten feet high, it was the smoothest sea that I had observed since July fourteenth.

We stayed on the water all that afternoon and all that night. The plane weathercocked into the wind, and the swells constantly hit the wing floats from the side. The Catalina creaked and groaned like an old haunted house. The waves engulfed the bow of the plane and broke against the hull. It was a tribute to our aircraft engineers that such a light structure as the hull of an airplane managed to withstand the merciless pounding of a heavy, angry sea.

I was indescribably grateful for companionship; and the courageous crewmen kept up a continual conversation with me, despite their seasickness.

At dawn of August fourth, the navigator reported that we were 100 miles due south of the enemy air base at Kahili on Bougainville. The waves were still ten feet high, but Hamblin decided to attempt a take-off nevertheless. He reasoned that if we stayed on the water, the plane would break up in the heavy sea. And the possibility of Jap strafing was always a threat. He felt that he had a 50-50 chance of getting the plane airborne. If the take-off failed, we would all be in the water that much sooner.

The take-off was successful! The cumbersome plane bounced off the tops of one swell and spanked onto another, knocking some rivets out of the hull. It bounced into the air about ten knots more slowly than it should have been to be airborne, but again Hamblin's skill saved our lives. No one but an expert pilot could have held that plane in the air without spinning. Hamblin was an expert, and we remained airborne.

Before taking off, Hamblin had lightened his ship by throwing every bit of loose gear overboard, saving just a very few rounds of ammunition for an emergency. He and his crew did an excellent job, for which they deserve the highest credit.

After we had been airborne about ten minutes, three more Catalinas appeared and escorted us home. They had come out to search for their lost plane. I was taken to a field hospital on Florida Island, where I stayed for three days. Then, shaving off my beard, I started my long trip home.

FOOD AND WATER

I suppose that by this time you are curious to know what I did for food and water. That is a story in itself, and I am going to tell it now.

When I landed on the sea, I had two days' emergency rations with me. These included six small cans of pemmican, three chocolate bars, a small jar of malted milk tablets, some multiple-vitamin tablets, some vitamin B1 tablets, and about three pints of water. I didn't eat a thing the first day. The second day I decided to ration my food to make it last at least twelve days. I allowed myself, therefore, four mouthfuls of water each day, half a chocolate bar, which I alternated every other day with one can of pemmican, two malted milk tablets, one multiple-vitamin tablet, and one vitamin B1 tablet.

On the fourth morning I found an eight-inch fish in my sea anchor. I didn't know how it had gotten there, but that didn't worry me. I took it out and ate it raw. All attempts to wring moisture out of the flesh failed.

On several occasions I speared fish with my sheath knife, for that was the only way I could catch them. They refused to take the baited hooks I hung on lines on the side of the raft. Tiny minnows appeared under the raft during the first few days and stayed there until I was rescued. I made a seine out of mosquito netting, caught some of the minnows, and swallowed them alive. I had always ridiculed the college boys who gained notoriety by swallowing live goldfish, but I guess now they must have been hungry, because it can be done if a fellow is hungry enough.

I kept my .45 in fairly good condition by "field stripping" and cleaning it every day. At first I lubricated it with sea water. After the first week I greased it with fatty tissue from birds.

I shot many birds during the twenty days, most of them "brown boobies," goose-like birds with a five-foot wing span. I ate the liver and drank the blood. The rest of the meat was not as palatable as the liver; but I cut in into very small pieces, chewed, and swallowed it. I had to force it down, but I knew in my mind that my body was getting nourishment.

When I shot the birds late in the afternoon after they had been fishing all day, they had fish in their throats. These fish were predigested to some extent. They stomach juices had started to work on them, and the meat was tender. I could pull it away from the bones, chew it, and swallow it. It tasted as though it had been partially cooked. It was perhaps the best thing I had to eat outside of my regular rations.

Before I ran out of fresh water, I decided to experiment with drinking sea water. I tried to rig a distilling apparatus out of two canteens, but it was unsuccessful. I tried using halazone tablets (they purify polluted water), but they have never purified sea water, and they never will. I tried iodine in the water, but that, of course, did not work. I didn't expect it to, but I had nothing to lose by trying. I even tried putting sulfanilamide in the water. Not being a chemist, I thought by some miracle that it might precipitate the salt. It did not.

My malted milk tablets were in a small jar with a metal cap of the "screw-on" type. I rigged a valve on the cap that would open under pressure. Securing the bottle to my fish line, I lowered it into the water. The valve opened at about a 40-foot depth and admitted water. I had two reasons for doing this: first of all I thought that the water at that depth, being under terrific pressure, might not have as much salt in the solution as the water at the surface and I might be able to drink it. Secondly, I thought that it might be colder than the water at the surface and that the bottle might sweat in the sun, like a pitcher of ice water, allowing me to lick the sweat off the bottle. Both assumptions were false, and the experiment was entirely unsuccessful.

One day I saw a "booby bird" land on the water, dip its long neck under the surface, and take a drink. It made me angry. I couldn't understand why the bird, which was only flesh and blood like myself, could drink sea water while I could not. I shot the bird, retrieved him quickly, and cut him open to trace the course of the water through his digestive system. There wasn't a thing unusual about it. The water just went in his mouth, down his throat, and into his stomach. Around the intestines of the "booby birds" I found a handful of fat, which I used for greasing my gun. One day the thought occurred to me that I might grease my mouth with the fat and get sea water into my stomach without tasting the salt. I did that. I greased my mouth, swallowed some to grease my throat, esophagus, and stomach, and drank sea water until the grease was washed away. For five days I drank a pint of water each day without ill effects. On the night of August second, when I capsized, I swallowed enough salt water to become nauseated. When I got back on the raft, I felt like vomiting. I got out some of the bird's fat and swallowed it. My stomach was settled immediately.

On the night of July twenty-sixth, it rained continuously all night. I laboriously filled my canteens. I caught the rain water in my sea anchor, but couldn't pour it into the canteen because of the rough sea. I finally solved that problem by putting the water in my mouth, then filling the canteen like a mother robin feeding its young. When the canteen was full, it was still raining, and I caught another cup of water, which I drank, thus ending the sea water experiment.

Although my rations were meager, I was able to keep my body in fairly good condition. I lost twenty pounds during the twenty days. I did suffer somewhat from pressure sores that developed on my elbows, my back, and my buttocks. On the raft, my feet were wrinkled and white from constant immersion in the salt water. After I was rescued, my hands, feet, and ankles began to swell. When the rescue plane hit the beach, I was unable to walk. There was absolutely no feeling from the waist down.

After three days in the field hospital, I was strong enough to start the journey homeward. My squadron was about four days ahead of me. They had left Guadalcanal and were already on their way home.

Thus ended an exciting experience in which I literally drifted into the "valley of the shadow of death" and out again.

EPILOGUE

What a story this pilot had to tell—and he would tell it at home, too: he was rescued just as his unit was shipping back to the States. But while he suffered his ordeal, the ecosystem of the ocean literally unfolded before his eyes. Birds, fish, whales, minnows, sailfish. The albatross was, of course, key; and he used it to survive. The albatross (also known as the gooney bird) resembles a North American seagull but it's much larger—one of the largest of all birds—with a wingspan of up to 12 feet. It's found mainly in the Southern Hemisphere and the South Atlantic, but not in North Atlantic, and it's not native to North America. Nonetheless, the pilots were trained to identify the bird and knew its stomach might contain food. Several survivors described their encounters with the albatross and how the fish in their bellies kept them alive. Largely because of that, the next generation of air-sea rescue planes would be named the Grumman SA-16 Albatross.

3

B-29 Down (the First B-29 to Ditch in World War II)

B-29 aircraft #304 of the 395th Bomb Sq. took off at 2359Z, 4 June 44, in accordance with F. O. #2, 58th Bomb Wing, dated 2 June 1944. On returning alone from the mission, this ship was forced to ditch at approximately 0940Z at 20°50'N - 88°00'N. Mechanical failure of the fuel transfer system necessitated ditching when the gas supply in the wing tanks was exhausted.

At the time of ditching, the personnel of the airplane consisted of 12 men (11 combat crew members and 1 passenger). Ten men were rescued and two combat crew men were lost.

The survivors were returned to the 112th Station Hospital, APO #465, New York City. The following are the individual statements of the survivors.

****

Co-Pilot—2nd Lt. A. L. Briggs

We'd had trouble with our transfer system prior to the mission, but thought that this problem had now been remedied. We were about two hours away (approx. 0715Z) from the target when we had our first indication of trouble, which was smoke coming from the Engineer's panel. The

Engineer attempted to fix the system and succeeded for a short time, but then the system burned completely out.

At the first sign of trouble the fuel gauges were checked and it was found that #1 engine was the lowest of the four and would be the first to go. Power was reduced on all engines and we let down from 15,000' to 10,000' so we could depressurize and get back in the ship and work. Enough air speed was kept up so the ship wouldn't rush along and, therefore, use more gas in the long run. The IAS was at all times between 165 MPH and 185 MPH.

One hour later (0815Z) we realized that we probably wouldn't be able to make land so the pilot gave the crew instructions to make preparations for ditching. All loose equipment was put in the forward bomb bay on the catwalk; however, the pilot gave instructions to move it off onto the bomb bay doors to prevent it from sliding forward through the hatch on impact. All personnel were instructed to fill their canteens and to take what equipment they would need for survival at sea. A five gallon water jug was filled to take with us.

In forty-five minutes (0900Z) #1 engine started cutting out so it was feathered. Power was increased on the other three and we started losing altitude at approximately 200' a minute to maintain our air speed. Everything was normal for five minutes, then #3 began cutting out. We knew it still had gas so we nursed it along. It would have a surge of power and then drag. This went on for thirty minutes. Then it had to be feathered. An attempt was made to unfeather the engine but it was unsuccessful.

We realized then that only with the best of luck would we make land. The ship was indicating approximately 150 MPH and pulling forty inches of manifold pressure and 2300 RPM. The pilot then ordered the bomb bay tanks to be emptied through the butterfly cocks and allowed to leak through the bomb bay doors. He also ordered the ammunition to be expended to make the ship as light as possible. He later stopped expending the ammunition when he realized the danger from the gas fumes in the plane. The crew members at their ditching stations complained of the gas fumes so I ordered the left gunner to open the rear escape hatch to give them more air. The ship flew normally for 10 minutes and the #4 cut out. The pilot immediately shut off all power and started down. The sea was calm and there were only a few white caps. The crew was alerted and the alarm bell turned on. The pilot called for full flaps at 130 IAS. The tail touched just lightly once at 105 IAS and a few seconds later a little harder. The pilot then closed his window. A moment later we hit the water for the third and final time. There was a terrible grinding and crumbling noise as the nose went under water. I was thrown forward against the armor plate glass; however, I had my seat cushion in front of my head and I attribute this to saving my life.

The nose filled with water immediately so I think the nose broke up. I reached up and pulled myself through the window and took four to six strokes to reach the surface. I saw that the life rafts had not been pulled so I crawled up on the wing and released the doors for the right raft which did not inflate so I had to pull the CO_2 bottle on this one. I gave this raft to the Engineer and then went to release the left raft. I also had to pull the CO_2 bottle on this one since it did not automatically inflate. I had a hard time getting the dinghy away from the airplane. I tried to untie the paddles, but the rope was knotted so I chewed it in two. With the aid of the paddles, I was able to clear the plane. The tail section had broken off just behind the gunner's compartment and was being held on to the major portion of the ship by a few control cables. The other crew members informed me that there was an explosion in the rear bomb bay, but I was not aware of it. I picked up three men in my dinghy and the Engineer also picked up three men. We got the two dinghies together and sighted two other men about 1000 yards away, who we identified as the Radar Operator and Left Gunner. Both boats tried to reach them until dark and then gave up the job as hopeless against the rising sea and tide. I had seen another B-29 make a 180° turn over us off to the right as I was climbing onto the wing so we expected to be picked up at least by noon the next day.

We settled down for the night and took stock of what equipment we had, which was as follows: 5 cans of water, 1 canteen of water, 1 jungle kit, 1 life vest (with medical supplies, food, and miscellaneous survival equipment), 3 E-3 Kits, 2 cans of hard sugar candy, and 1 "Gibson Girl." We figured we could last a long time if we could just get more water.

I took off the cover of the Gibson Girl, tied a rope to it, and shoved it down in the water with the oar, and found that it made a very good sea anchor. During the night we had to weather two short squalls—one at about 1130Z and the other at 2000Z. We held the dinghies abeam with the oars laced through the rubber rings on each raft. We were afraid that the rough sea would upset our boats if we tied them in trail. All crew members, with the exception of the Engineer and myself, appeared to be visibly shaken from the explosion in the rear of the ship. Everyone bedded down as best he could with the exception of myself and I sat up and prayed that everything would turn out O.K.

We had seen a buoy just before nightfall and decided that in the morning we would try to tie onto it, provided we were in the same vicinity. Approximately at daybreak (6 June, '44) we sighted a buoy, but in view of the two squalls we had been through I do not think that it was the same buoy. We rowed up to it. We then tried to use our Gibson Girl radio. It was too calm to fly the kite and the balloons had been lost so we separated the rafts and extended the antenna between them. We were getting current, but got no indication we were "putting out." The SOS signal was cranked out 15 minutes before then 15 minutes after the hour and then we cranked steady for about an hour.

We were beginning to need water because the hot sun and rowing we were doing made us very thirsty. We rationed our water from the beginning, but the supply was now getting very low. At 0400Z that morning I sighted something that was either land or a boat in the horizon so we eagerly started rowing and sailing toward it. We tried to reach land for about 5 hours and then gave up very tired and dejected because the tide was carrying us out faster than we could row and sail. We knew this to be true because the Navigator had started fishing and the line would trail in the direction we were trying to move.

At this time we sighted two objects to our right bobbing in the water and decided to go investigate. As we got within 200 yards we saw it was the two crew members (Radar Operator and Left Gunner) we had failed to reach the day before. The Left Gunner was holding the Radar Operator's head out of water by pushing him up on an oxygen bottle they had picked up floating in the water. The Left Gunner said he was O.K. and to get the Lieutenant out of the water first because he was injured seriously. We pulled the Radar Operator into the boat and started to attend to his wounds with the drugs and bandages from the Engineer's life vest. He had a compound fracture of the left leg. Two leg bones were sticking through the calf of his leg and there was a hole about an inch square in the top of his knee straight down to the bone. The right leg also had a hole in it on the inside of his ankle through which the ankle bone was visible. His right arm was obviously broken and he complained of his left hip, which we later found out from the doctor was broken. He was delirious from pain and was obviously out of his head. The Engineer poured an excess of sulfanilamide powder into all his wounds and used the compresses and bandages that were available from the vest. A splint was made for his leg out of one set of oars to prevent the bones from grinding together and causing him terrible pain. The Engineer then gave him a styrette of morphine and this seemed to make him rest easier for a few hours.

To our surprise we found that the Left Gunner had three large cuts in the back of his neck and lacerations over the top of his head. One of the deep cuts in his neck only missed the large artery in the right side of his neck by about 1/8 of an inch. This artery was plainly visible through the gash. The left upper arm was also gashed, exposing the bone. The Engineer also poured an excess of sulfanilamide powder in his wounds and bandaged them with his first aid equipment. The Left Gunner undoubtedly did one of the most wonderful jobs of self sacrifice beyond the call of duty that I know of, in holding the Radar Operator afloat for approximately 24 hours. This opinion is shared with me by all crew members.

We decided to separate the dinghies about 1300Z and let each group try to reach shore individually. I took the Engineer, Radar Operator, Left Gunner and Tail Gunner with me. Both dinghies became separated after about 3 miles. At dark I realized we weren't making any headway so we decided to make ourselves as comfortable as possible. We had given the rest of our water to the two wounded men and now everyone was suffering miserably from thirst. We had been eating the candy charms from the Engineer's vest and the life raft, and they helped relieve our thirst a great deal.

Approximately at midnight I felt a NW wind coming up so I roused the men and we put up our sail and were going to try to make land. At 2100Z we were getting very close because we could hear the waves beating on the mud banks. As we neared them we saw they were six to eight feet high. The Engineer and I prayed together that we would wash over the banks on a crest of a high wave so our boat would not be overturned and the Radar

Operator suffer more pain. We floated up high and dry on the bank. We then started unloading the wounded men and supplies. We dropped the Radar Operator and he screamed in pain, which I assure you hurt us as much as it did him. He was delirious again since the morphine had worn off, and we had no more. We built a fire and made ourselves as comfortable as possible for the night. We covered the two wounded men with the sail. We all slept around the fire because it was chilly.

That morning about 2300Z, the Engineer and Tail Gunner went to look for an Indian they thought they saw. The Left Gunner set up the Gibson Girl and cranked out an SOS. This time there was an indication that he was putting out. He cranked the radio 15 minutes before and 15 minutes after the hour and then cranked steady for about an hour. The Engineer and the Tail Gunner returned at approximately 0300Z (7 June '44) with no results. Everyone was suffering terribly from thirst. I and the Tail Gunner then took off on a search for 3 hours and still found no water or natives. We would taste the water in small inland pools, but it was all salty. It was about noon now and very hot. The Radar Operator had rolled over on his face in the sand and was very delirious. He kept asking for water so we decided we would have to get some. I then tried distilling salt water. We took the rubber hose off a Mae West and attached it to the oxygen bottle we had filled with salt water. We then boiled the water and caught the steam in a plastic water bottle on the other end of the rubber hose. We poured cool sea water on the water bag to help condense the steam. It was very hot work but we managed to get about 1/2 a pint of water this way. We gave the water to the Radar Operator. It was brackish, but not too bad. We made a tent for the 2 wounded men out of the sail, for the purpose of keeping them out of the sun. We used the maps out of our money belts and life vests as wet rags for the heads of the two wounded men. We kept them as moist as possible as a means of keeping them cool. The maps also came in handy for this operation. The rest of us would lay in the cool water on the mud flats and this helped us a great deal.

The Engineer and I told the Tail Gunner that we were going to look for help and wouldn't return until we found aid. The Tail Gunner was to look after the two wounded men.

We walked up the beach about 5 miles and didn't find a thing. We decided to lay in the water awhile and rest. While we were resting we sighted a native and both of us started toward him smiling and waving to him. He smiled back and we gave him 3 silver rupees. He could not speak English but through motions and the word "Pani" he knew what we wanted. We followed him for approximately 3 miles to a little pool. He brushed the scum off the water and rinsed his mouth and told us to do the same which we did. He then took us on to a village, where we were given drinking water and food. We used halazone tablets in the water and drank our fill. A native who was obviously the Chief in the area came to us and spoke broken English. We learned from him that we were on an island near the mouth of the Hooghly River. We told him there were 3 others (2 seriously wounded) and told him where they were. He got his boat and we went after them. We made a stretcher for the Radar Operator by cutting the oval ends out of one life raft and sticking poles through it. We then put two cross bars between the carrying poles to hold the stretcher taut. The natives then carried him about 7 miles to a native hospital where a native doctor dressed his wounds again. The doctor took the Engineer's life vest and cut up the vest, taking out all the medicines and equipment, which we were now glad to give to him. The Engineer, Tail Gunner, and I went back to the native village, where the Indians were preparing a fish dinner for us, with fried rice. It was now almost 1600Z when a native came in saying he had sighted 5 other men not far away. We got in the boat and picked up the other men in our crew. We carried water to them in the plastic water bottle and native jugs and used halazone tablets in the water. We all returned to the village and went to sleep. The next day we were picked up by a PBY, which we signaled with a flash mirror. The Indians had sent for help by sending a runner 18 miles to Diamond Harbor on the Hooghly River, where a radio message was sent to ASR in Calcutta.

NAVIGATOR—1ST LT. J. W. EVANS

The Pilot instructed the Radio Operator to turn on the IFF to the very wide or #3 position. I furnished him with a position report for 0901Z of 20° 07'N - 89° 00'E. Before I was ordered to my ditching station I furnished him with a position report for 0931Z but I do not know whether he ever sent it. Everyone was unbelievably calm and crew discipline was excellent.

I braced myself against the armor plate wall in the front of the radar compartment. I put on a summer flying helmet sideways so the earphone compartments guarded the front and back of my head. I then wrapped a B-10 flying jacket around my head and held my head back against the wall so there would be no snap of my neck on impact. I had a B-10 flying jacket on with 2 E-3 Sustenance kits in the side pockets as well as a full canteen of water and a Carlisle First Aid Packet. The gas fumes in the rear of the ship were suffocating us so the Left Gunner opened the rear escape hatch.

I remember the ship touched the water twice lightly and then everything is blank. I think we exploded because I found myself in the water near the airplane. There was yellow flame and smoke in the bomb bays for approximately 30 seconds. I was stunned and very weak. I inflated my Mae West and decided to let them pick me up in the life raft, but I began to drift away so I swam to the dinghy the Engineer was paddling. My field jacket with E-3 kits had been blown off and only the arms were left. We tried to pick up the Radar Operator and Left Gunner, but were unable to do so before dark in the rising sea and tide.

I had a miserable night in the dinghy because my left arm was paining me and I thought it was broken. It rained about 1400Z but we did not bother about catching water because we believed we had been sighted and would be picked up the next day. I started to eat a D-ration bar and some malted milk dextrose tablets that night that the Engineer gave me, but stopped because they made me thirsty.

The next day was uneventful except for picking up the Radar Operator and Left Gunner, which the Co-Pilot has already told you about. I tried fishing for about an hour, but had no luck. When we sighted land and started paddling toward it we saw we were actually going backwards faster than we would paddle forward because my fishing line was dragging in front of the boat.

When we separated the two dinghies I had the Bombardier, Senior Gunner, Right Gunner and Passenger with me. We were about a mile ahead and a mile to the right of the other dinghy when we decided to give up and bed down for the night. I noticed a strong northerly wind coming up so we put up our sail about 0800Z and sailed into shore about 2100Z. We tried to start a fire with our matches from the E-3 Kits but they had gotten damp. The other dry matches the Engineer had, so we buried ourselves in the sand to keep warm and went to sleep.

The next morning (7 June '44) I had walked down the beach about a mile and found one inland river. The tide was running in and the wind was with us so we all got in the dinghy and expected to sail up this river to a native village. We passed a single straw hut, but went on thinking we could find more life. We sailed until approximately 0800Z when the river came to an end and we found nothing. The Bombardier caught 3 crabs and we ate them. This helped our thirst a bit, but not much. On the way back we stopped at the thatched hut we had seen before and looked for life, but found none. We stayed there too long because the tide stopped going out toward to sea and we had to row back approximately five miles to where we had landed the night before. We were all very thirsty and the candy charms we had relieved our thirst a great deal. We were tired and really slept well that night. About 1800Z we got up to catch rain water, but though heavy clouds passed us by it failed to rain. About 2200Z we heard a whistle and it was the five men from the other dinghy coming in a native boat to pick us up. We went to the native village and had a delicious meal and rested until a PBY came and picked us up. While in the village we learned that the matches in the E-3 kit were safety matches and the striker was on the inside of the top. The E-3 kits should be waterproof because everything was ruined with the possible exception of the matches.

ENGINEER—2ND LT. J. E. PHALEN

I had 150 feet of electric wire along so I tried to partially rewire the transfer system and it worked for a few minutes. I then completely rewired the system and it worked for a few minutes again. However, it burned out for good this time and nothing could be done.

The Pilot asked to be wired into his seat, which I did, but later I understand the Co-Pilot talked him out of this plan. I was wearing a homemade vest with first aid equipment, food, survival equipment, etc. I also had ready to take with me a full canteen of water, an ex, and a first aid kit. I braced myself for the impact with my head against the armor plate. We touched the water twice very lightly and I cut the switches just before the final impact. The pilot did a fine job of landing the ship. The water rushed in so fast that I just had time to get myself out. I had nothing with me except the home-made life vest I had on.

The Radio Operator was next to me, braced against the armor plate by the Co-Pilot. He moved after the second slight touch. I put my hand on his shoulder to restrain him, but was unsuccessful. He was getting up to pull the life raft releases. I am almost sure the upper forward turret cover is what hit him.

I climbed up on the wing and the Co-Pilot gave me a life raft and I started picking up the crew. I ran across the Gibson Girl Radio floating in the water so I put it in the dinghy. We tried to reach the Radar Operator and Left Gunner, but were unable to because of the high sea. While we were trying to reach them I looked back and saw the ship go under. It stayed up about 20 minutes. The severed tail section sank first.

The rest of the experience is just as the Co-Pilot has related. I wish to say, however, that we would have been in a bad way if we had not had the medi-cines and the life vest I was wearing. I feel that this vest had a great deal to do with saving two boys' lives. This seems to be the most logical way to carry escape and survival equipment. For example, when I got out of my escape hatch I had both hands free to work and not full of miscellaneous equipment. The book on survival at sea in the vest was a great help. I took a suggestion for distilling water from it when on land and it worked with only meager success, but it was worth it. I wet a sock with sea water and stuffed it in the mouth of the plastic water bottle and then poured cool sea water on the outside of the bag. I got a little water, but not much. I mixed it with the lemon extract powders I had and this made it taste better. Probably, if I had worked longer I would have gotten more water, but the steam we were dis-tilling from the heated water in the oxygen bottle was a better method so I gave up. The candy charms are very good for thirst and seem to relieve a "cotton mouth" almost immediately.

BOMBARDIER—1ST LT. B. F. WOPTIKA

I placed my Navigation brief case in front of the bomb site to prevent it from snapping off and going through the nose of the ship. I then wrapped my B-10 flying jacket around the bomb site. I went to my ditching station in the gunner's compartment and braced myself against the bulkhead leading into the bomb bay. I locked my hands behind my head and put my head and elbows between my knees. The gas fumes were intense just before we hit. I had an E-3 kit in my pocket and a full canteen of water on a web belt. However, when the ship exploded and I went down in the water, I lost them. I came up under the bomb bays and saw yellow flames and smoke so I ducked under the water and swam clear of the ship. I was the first man in the Engineer's raft.

The rest of the story is the same as the others have told. I want to mention, however, that the candy charms are a great relief from thirst and that I worked almost all night the first night on land to dig a well. I got it about arm's length deep, but got no water. I rested a few hours and when I went back it was full of salt water.

O.F.C. Gunner—Sgt. N. E. Belcher

I braced myself against the rear bomb bay bulkhead and held my hands behind my head and my elbows and head between my knees. I had a pistol, full canteen of water, knife, and an E-3 kit. The gas fumes in the rear of the ship were very nauseating before the ship exploded. I must have gone through the bottom because I found myself in the water about 15 yards from the airplane. I inflated my Mae West and waited until I was picked up. My canteen of water did not have a cork stopper in the cover and as a result it was full of salt water and gasoline. The Engineer thought it was best that we get rid of the water so we wouldn't be tempted to drink it later when we were thirsty, so we poured it out.

The rest of the experience is just as the others have said. I ate malted milk dextrose tablets and a D-ration bar the Engineer gave me from his vest, the first night on the water. The D-ration bar and tablets I had in my E-3 kit were salty and soggy, because the kit was not water proof. I was afraid to eat these for fear they would make me thirsty. The waterproof medicines and concentrated food the Engineer had certainly saved us.

I wish to say the natives certainly treated us well and should be rewarded for their hospitality in some way.

LEFT GUNNER—SGT. W. W. WISEMAN

I was not in my proper ditching position because the Co-Pilot had ordered me to open the rear escape hatch so we could get some relief from the heavy gas fumes that were in the ship. I opened the escape hatch and had started back to my position when I felt the tail lightly touch the water. Realizing that I might not have enough time to get to my post, I lay down on one of the cots in the radar compartment and braced myself for the impact as best I could. I held my head as solid as possible against the cot framework. From here on everything is blank. The other crew members told me I was blown out of the ship. I remember I was under water so I swam to the top, but must have passed out again because I again found myself under water. I inflated my Mae West and came to the surface. I know I was very weak and really don't remember what happened for quite some time. I did see the dinghy and thought they were coming to pick me up. I never realized that they were having a hard time reaching me. Night came on and I heard someone hollering so I yelled also. I found out it was the Radar Operator. I told him to keep yelling and we would be able to get together. We almost bumped heads before we realized we were so close. He had found an oxygen bottle from the ship and had it under his arm. The heavy sea we were having at this time was responsible for his taking in so much salt water. The position he had assumed on the oxygen bottle was causing him to take in a lot more water than was necessary (the Radar Operator does not know how to swim) so I told him to take it out from under his arm and straighten up in the water. This he did. He kept complaining of the pain he was suffering and that he thought he was going to drown in the high sea. The squall grew more intense and the waves tossed the Radar Operator around so he could not catch his breath. I had him hold the oxygen bottle at both ends with his hands and then I would grab him around the waist and push him up on the bottle. The collar of his Mae West would catch on the bottle and he would ride this way for a few minutes and be quiet. I was unable to hold him up like this for more than a few minutes because the waves would prevent me from breathing while they were breaking so fast. I would then let him go while I caught my breath. He would start screaming again so I kept repeating this operation. (The Left Gunner weighs approximately 125 pounds, the Radar Operator weighs approximately 160 pounds.) I was getting tired so I dropped my shoes and full canteen of water. I figured that the canteen the Radar Operator was wearing would be enough for both of us. After we were in the water a few hours crabs began eating on my neck and arm and the Radar Operator's legs. I could brush them off fairly well, but they caused my companion a great deal of pain. They just wouldn't leave us alone. I think this had a great deal to do with his becoming delirious.

Just shortly after we had weathered our second squall during the first night, the Radar Operator went out of his head and was delirious from the pain of his injuries. We had just taken a drink from his canteen when he pulled his knife out and went to kill us both. I was very scared and was afraid he might succeed. I had more strength left than he did and managed to get it away from him. He also wanted to pull his Mae West off. I had lost a lot of strength by now and if he hadn't decided to quiet down I think he would have finished us both.

A little afternoon we were picked up by the dinghies. At this time I found out about the cuts in my neck, head, and arm. I was not aware of them before. I don't remember much of what happened from then on because I was pretty groggy. The candy charms helped my thirst a good deal. I understand if the Engineer had not had that life vest with the waterproof drugs I might have gotten blood poisoning and lost my life. This seems to be the best way to carry essential supplies.

Epilogue

This is an historically interesting report because it is the first ditching of the new B-29. The incident also occurred during the first mission ever for the 58th Bomb Wing. The 58th was based in India and had been sent out to bomb a Japanese rail yard in Thailand. The mission was to be the longest ever of the war— 2,261 miles—but it did not go well. Twenty-two B-29s turned back before reaching Thailand; 42 diverted or crashed for fuel-related causes on the way home, including the crew of this bomber, which went in with all hands on board.

This incident is also unique in that it is told from the perspective of six different crew members. The crew recognized they made some critical mistakes before hitting the water, which they included in their comments.

The B-29 had teething problems as it entered service. Its engines were unreliable and the turbochargers often caught fire.

The B-29 carried a crew of 11, although this crew also carried an extra pas-senger.

4

Whistle in the Night

This short but incredibly dramatic story is a portrait of war most fiercely fought—observed by a downed pilot floating in the Pacific Ocean in the middle of the largest and most intense naval sea battle in American history.

****

One shrill blast from a small, police-type whistle was responsible for the rescue of a U. S. Navy pilot who repeatedly dodged death after being shot down during the Battle of Leyte Gulf.

The American was one of four carrier-based fighter pilots launched to attack a Japanese surface formation consisting of one heavy cruiser and three new heavy destroyers. Japanese five-inch and 40-mm fire caused the four-plane flight to split and make the attack through a heavy cumulonimbus layer which was 2,000 to 8,000 feet thick.

The death-cheating pilot broke through the cloud and came out on the right side of the cruiser. Almost immediately, 18 inches of the plane's right wing was shot off.

He pressed his strafing run to point blank range, dropped his right wing tank and then pulled out toward cloud cover.

On the pull-out, a Jap Pete flew in front of him and the American fired. When last seen, the Pete was smoking.

Just before reaching the cloud, a Jap five-inch shell burst in front of and underneath the Navy fighter and blew off the cowl and hatch.

The windscreen was broken, one of the propeller blades was torn off and the pilot received minor injuries. He was then in the middle of the cloud and took a heading for his escort carrier. When the American emerged from the cloud he was over the three Jap heavy destroyers. They fired at the Yank until he hit the water. As he descended, the engine went out and the plane merely glided toward the water.

JAP SHELL FLOATING AIRPLANE

Shoulder straps prevented the pilot's being injured on hitting the water. After recovering from the initial shock, the Yank pilot heard a loud explosion behind him. One of the destroyers had blown off half the plane's tail with 40-mm ammunition. Before he could get out of the aircraft, another Jap shell landed right behind the cockpit. He abandoned the plane immediately and lacked time to take a life raft with him. The Japs blew up the airplane a short time later. A U. S. destroyer, a unit of a nearby task force, made one attempt to rescue the American, but heavy shelling by the Jap surface craft forced the destroyer to withdraw. As the Jap naval force proceeded southward, the cruiser passed to the left of the downed American and a destroyer to the right. The vessels disappeared over the horizon.

About an hour later, a Jap Frances arrived at the crash site. The Jap pilot made four strafing runs on the American pilot, apparently strafing until ammunition was exhausted. During each strafing attack the American submerged by leaving his life jacket on the surface and diving about 10 feet under the surface towards the attacking plane. When the action broke off, the Jap flew low over the area and wagged his wings. Some time later, a Japanese surface force approached. Two battleships and a heavy cruiser passed fairly close to the American, who could see other Jap cruisers on the horizon.

Soon the American saw a Pete airplane and as there was no gunner in the rear cockpit he concluded that the Jap pilot wanted to pick him up as a prisoner. The Pete flew a series of figure-eights over the American, but apparently the Jap pilot did not see his prey. U. S. torpedo planes attacking the

Jap ships passed over the downed American. He observed five hits on the Jap heavy cruiser and watched it sink. The other Jap ships left the area.

Just before dark, two Jap destroyers appeared to the north and four Wildcats began strafing them. Two of the Wildcats were shot down; one struck the water about 100 feet from the downed American. The other two Wildcats returned and circled the spot. The American dropped his last dye marker, but it was not noticed by the airborne Wildcat pilots.

After swimming all night (the American learned that even with his life jacket on it was necessary to swim to keep his mouth and nose out of the water), a U. S. destroyer passed him three hours after sunrise. The weary survivor realized the men on the destroyer had not seen him and he blew a blast on his whistle. The destroyer turned and picked up the water-logged pilot. Later he was transferred to a vessel travelling to Ulithi.

EPILOGUE

There is never a good time to be shot down, but doing so in the middle of the largest sea battle in naval history certainly takes the cake. The Battle of Leyte Gulf took place in the Philippine Sea near the islands of Leyte, Samar, and Luzon. The Japanese would lose 28 ships and some 300 aircraft; the Americans and Australians would see six ships sink and 200 airplanes go down, including one that crashed into the sea near this pilot. Some 12,000 Japanese would lose their lives, while Allied casualties would number more than 2,500. The battles raged for four days in October of 1944.

5

A COOL HEAD IN A RUBBER BOAT

U.S. Pacific Fleet Air Force Operations Memorandum No. 46 tells the gripping tale of an American airman who was shot down on 11 June while participating in a fighter sweep over Tinian. The intensity of the combat is notable—even as he went down, the flames that engulfed his wings were so intense that they started cooking off his belts of ammunition. When he finally went in, his survival training kicked in much to his benefit. He spent 80 hours alone at sea in a rubber raft.

****

Whitworth's adventures began when a Jap bullet splattered into the instrument panel of his F6F and another Jap bullet spanged into his starboard wing and kindled a flame in the gas tank. Whitworth went into a steep drive at 8,000 feet and tried to jettison his hood, without success (possibly because of his speed). The flames in his wings began to fire his guns and he expected the aircraft to explode at any moment. He reached the water before this occurred and made a successful landing.

His plane started to sink immediately, nose first. He had his parachute harness on and it caught on the canopy while he was trying to get free of the cockpit under water. He managed to get clear and surfaced in time to observe that the Zeke had followed him down. Whitworth took no chances on the Jap's humanitarian instincts and promptly dived. When he came up again the Zeke had gone.

Whitworth's parachute and back pack were buoyant and held him up while he inflated the life raft, which functioned perfectly. He was able to salvage all of his equipment except a bottle of water which he had in the cockpit. He had two other containers of water (cans), a sheath knife, an extra pair of summer flying gloves, an extra handkerchief, a tube of camphor ice, sunglasses, notebook and pencils, chewing gum, waterproof map of the area, .38 revolver, plus oil in an old CO2 cartridge and a well stocked first aid kit.

As soon as he got into the raft, Whitworth secured most of his inventory in the raft pockets and lashed the rest with lines. It is fortunate that he took this precaution because at dusk of the first day, a Betty flew directly overhead at 300 feet and he had to overturn the raft (blue bottom up) to avoid detection. While the sun was still high he avoided sunburn by the following precautions: his summer flying suit did not quite cover his ankles and wrists, so he cut off pieces of parachute and wrapped them around the exposed areas. He pulled his overseas cap down over his ears and wrapped his neck and lower face with the parachute cloth. He kept his sunglasses on and put sulfathiazole ointment on the exposed tip of his nose. As a result, he was unharmed by the sun.

The waves broke over the raft and kept him drenched. When the sun went down he became chilled. It was necessary to bail every hour. The raft had a leak he couldn't detect. He went without sleep all night and the raft capsized once.

At dawn on 12th June, enemy planes rendezvoused overhead, and instead of turning over his raft he covered himself with blue sail cloth. During the day he checked his gear and found out that much of it had been damaged by salt water, even though wrapped in condoms. His marine flashlight was ruined and his Navy wristwatch stopped. He had a penlight wrapped in rubber, and water also got into this the next day, rendering the battery defective. At that time he took the precaution of removing the extra battery and bulb in his back pack from the tin foil (because he was afraid the tin foil might puncture the rubber) and rewrapped it in some extra condoms. It is his feeling that this single precaution may have saved his life. As another precaution he removed his hunting knife because the point had slipped through the sheath and he was afraid it might puncture the raft, which he was extremely careful to protect.

The rest of the story follows in his own words:

"That afternoon I saw the first shark; it was only about four feet long. It swam around and under the raft, his fin rubbing against me as he passed under. Later on, several more appeared but they did not bother me. They were eating some small fish that had been attracted to the gear hanging from the raft.

"As soon as I realized that I would not drift ashore on Tinian, I put my sea anchor out in order to stay as close as possible to land. This kept the raft into the wind but did not keep it from drifting, and the jerk on the line made it ship more water than before. I lengthened the line on the sea anchor and also put some parachute over it, and this seemed to help a little.

"Late in the afternoon I took my first swallow of water after eating a couple of malted milk tablets. I had purposely kept from eating or drinking for 24 hours as we had been instructed to do this. Besides, I felt no real hunger or thirst and chewed gum constantly, which kept my mouth moist. At dusk the coast of Tinian was about 20 miles away, and this was the last time I saw land.

"The next morning, the 13th, I saw a group of friendly aircraft, but they were too high to spot me. I was still drifting steadily north-west. During the day I tried a little fishing, but had no luck. In the afternoon an albatross tried to land on the raft. I sat very still and hoped to catch it, but it kept slipping off the wet rubber, and finally landed in the water, about eight feet away. I shot it through the breast, skinned it and ate part of it raw, although I wasn't very hungry. The bird did not bleed at all, but the meat was red and tough. I chewed it for a long time and then spat out the fiber. There were four small fish in the stomach, and I ate three of them. They were partly digested and tasted pretty good—about like half-cooked meat. I took the fourth fish and rubbed it against my feet, which were beginning to swell and get numb. I slapped my feet with gloves and the oil, and massaging them seemed to help them. I wrapped the wings and legs of the bird in parachute cloth and ate them the next day, even sucking the marrow out of the bones.

"That night it was very cold and the raft was still full of water. I could see some fires in the distance and thought we might have met the Jap fleet (these were sampans which our forces had attacked and destroyed). I knew that I was west of the last piece of land and drifting further out to sea. Very few aircraft had appeared overhead that day and I was getting a little discouraged. At the time I figured that I could last about 15 days provided the salt water didn't get me. My buttocks were already sore and itching, my elbows chapped, and my feet beginning to get numb.

"On the 14th, I saw no ships or aircraft. It rained once, but with the pitching of the raft, I was able to collect only a mouthful in the sailcloth. That night the sky was overcast and it was very dark. Just about the time I had got settled for the night I heard a rumbling noise, and looked around to see a large dark shape moving toward me. At first I thought it might be a storm, but later made out a battleship blowing its stacks. It passed within thirty yards of me and the wash almost upset the raft. I didn't know whether it was Jap or American, but as it passed I saw the silhouette of an OS2U airplane on the stern, and then I started yelling. Later a destroyer appeared, but my Very flares were wet and would not fire. I got the extra battery and bulb out and tried to put it in the flashlight, but in the dark and trying to hurry I was unable to put it together. Finally I got it to work by holding the bulb against the battery, and in a few minutes the can flashed an 'O.K.' and took me aboard. It was so dark that I am sure they would have missed me if I had not had the light. It turned out that the battleship had heard my calls, and thinking that a man was lost overboard had notified the destroyer to stand by.

"At the time of my rescue I had used four-fifths of a can of water and some malted milk tablets. All of my equipment worked fine and I'm sure sold on that back-pad. The worst hardship was that of being continually wet. It would be a big help if the sailcloth was a little larger and fastened with snap fasteners along the large end of the raft. Although this would not keep you dry, it would keep the water off your back at night. I read the pamphlet on survival many times and used some of the suggestions. I tried to signal with the mirror, but it didn't work, probably because the aircraft were too far away. Two days later I was ready to fly, my feet were O.K., I had no sores except a few spots on the cuticle of my nails, and the itch around my buttocks was improving. But I had time to do a lot of thinking out there, and I want to say it made a fox-hole preacher out of me."

6

ENEMY TACTICS

The P-38 Lightning was one of the most successful fighter aircrafts of World War II, proving to be particularly effective in the Pacific, where its long-range, concentrated firepower and agility helped turn more than 100 pilots into aces. Here, a P-38 pilot recounts a mission that nearly made him an ace, yet on his next mission he was shot down and repeatedly strafed. He ended up in the Pacific Ocean, near Pandan Point off of Leyte in the Surigao Strait, a hundred miles east of the major Japanese air base on Negros Island in the Philippines. When he was rescued he was flown down to the Allied air and sea base on the island of Morotai near New Guinea.

****

NOVEMBER 4, 1944

I was leading the squadron to cover B-24s over Alicante. After we reached the target area I circled a few times at 14,000 and observed one enemy fighter taking off from the strip. I dived down and he ducked in a cloud but I saw him come out and fired a 90° deflection, but was a little short on my lead. He rolled out of his turn and started to climb, with me following. He got up to about 4,000 feet and I was about to shoot when he did a slight turn. I fired a short burst and hit his right wing about three feet from the tip. He tightened his turn and I fired a full deflection, hitting him with a short burst in the cockpit. He started to burn and hit the water. This was an Oscar. I started to climb and an Oscar got on my tail. I made a turn and he started to fire. A P-38 opened up on him from a deflection shot and he started to burn and crashed. I then climbed to 7,000 feet and saw another Oscar dive into a cloud. I stayed below the cloud till he came out and he headed for the land west of the Alicante airdrome when I got in range. He was right down to the trees when I fired. But he turned and I got only a few hits in his wing tip. His left wing hit a tree and he exploded as he crashed. I climbed up to 6,000 feet and started south, about half-way between Alicante and Bacolod sighting a lone Oscar. He was very hard to hit as he kept pulling in tight turns and ducking in and out of clouds. I fired four bursts, all 45° to 90° deflection, getting a few hits each time. He finally burst into flames and crashed on land about 15 miles south of Alicante. I then started for home and was attacked by two Tonys which were 1,000 feet above me and to my left. I dived at full throttle and went through a cloud. That was the last I saw of them.

The enemy seemed very eager and to have a great deal more experience than they usually have.

NOVEMBER 7, 1944

We were on a B-24 escort mission to Alicante airdrome and upon reaching the target sighted an Oscar taking off. We headed down after it and the Oscar was destroyed by one of our pilots. We then circled around the area and upon sighting nothing headed for home. Another P-38 and I were alone and behind a bit. We were climbing up when three Tonys came from above and to the right. One got a pass and shot out my right engine. It started to smoke and then caught fire in spite of my efforts to control it. I called my wingman and told him I was bailing out, but didn't give position. I pulled up to 1,000 feet and bailed out over the vicinity of Pandan Point in Guimaras Strait. My chute opened at about 300 feet before I hit the water. I failed to see where my P-38 crashed, for a Tony was circling down on me and I kept my eye on him. When about 50 feet from water, he made a strafing pass on me but shot below. During this time three more had joined him. The second one started a pass when I was up about 80 feet off the water. I had my chute straps unbuckled so I immediately fell from the chute and the Tony could not get an accurate shot. After hitting the water, the other two came in and made passes. I swam under water away from the chute as much as possible. The Nips were more or less firing in the vicinity of the chute, therefore missing me. On the leader's second pass, he fired a burst and I ducked under water (as I had done on the previous passes). When I came up again he hadn't passed over me but saw me come up, so he pushed his nose down and tried to get another hit. He came too low and his prop hit the water and he went in, blowing up. The other three immediately broke off, reformed and circled about 5 minutes and then landed on Negros Island. About 10 minutes later, one Tony came back, circled and fired at my chute, then returned and landed again. A sail boat came out and picked up my chute, boat, pack and other articles. I had nothing but a Mae West which I kept deflated until I was well out in the bay.

I hit the water about a mile and a half south of Pandan Point and one-quarter-mile off shore. I worked my way south as much as possible so I could get on land close to the hills if I wasn't rescued the following day. During the night sail boats were out in the bay and around the shore. One passed within 50 yards of me and two men with rifles stood in it. I don't know if they were looking for me or not. It seems that after dark all boats had green sails.

At about 1800 hours single planes started passing over at about 10-15 minute intervals. All night I heard ships passing over. The ones I saw at day-break and dusk were Libbys. They all seemed to be coming from west of Negros Island.

At about 1100 hours on 5 November, I sighted P-38s coming up around the shore searching for me. I put out my sea marker and began swimming around to spread it. The P-38 failed to see me at first but on the next turn sighted me (through flashes from my mirror and through my sea marker). At 1135, a Catalina landed and picked me up. We then returned to Morotai.

7

FOX TARE CHARLIE

Because it was easy to see the hatches and cranes on the decks of Japanese cargo ships and freighters, Japanese ships were identified using code names based on the number of hatches seen. A Fox Tare Charlie was a medium class merchantman with four cargo holds and two booms. A Sugar Dog was a smaller 150-ton supply ship with one large hold. In this story, Navy aircraft were attacking Japanese coastal freighters when a cluster bomb prematurely exploded, leading to this tale of survival. This action took place in the Philippines. Narration is by Lieutenant (jg) J. S. McDonald, USNR, and Commander T. H. Winters, USN; the parenthetical comments in this report were inserted by the staff debriefer.

****

LT. (JG) J. S. McDONALD, USNR

Our strike group of 16 VF, 10 VS and 8 VT was launched against the Visayan Islands from the U.S.S. *Lexington* at 1400/I on 13 September 1944. After the rendezvous our strike group headed for Mactan Island, the assigned targets on which we had been briefed being the barracks area at Mactan airfield. However, the entire Mactan-Cebu area was closed in by weather and from the smoke pouring from oil storage tanks at Cebu which had been hit by earlier strikes. Therefore, the strike group proceeded to the northeast along the coast of Cebu, hoping to intercept any shipping that might have fled Cebu Harbor. We located two ships, a Fox Tare Charlie which was slightly damaged and appeared to be beached on a reef, and a Sugar Dog, off the northeast coast of Cebu and immediately attacked. The "Skipper", Lieut. Comdr. Dressendorfer, who was leading the VT attack, dove on the FTC. I was flying wing on his wing so I pushed over on the FTC, too, but as I could not get on the ship in my dive, I released only one frag cluster, which was wide of the ship. I regained altitude and made a second attack on the ship, releasing the other nine frag clusters, scoring a hit and several near misses which were observed by my radioman from the tunnel. However, a moment later two or three frag clusters exploded after leaving the bomb bay, lifting the aircraft violently in the air and riddling the fuselage and wings with fragments and blowing off part of the tail. Fortunately, my radioman was lying flat on his stomach in the tunnel in a position to fire on our pull-out when the explosion occurred, and he was protected by the armor plating which probably saved his life. My hydraulic line was damaged. However, I was able to close the bomb bay doors. Then I saw that my oil pressure was falling rapidly and I realized it was time to look around for a spot to make a forced landing. I called our strike leader, Commander Winters, over VHF, saying that I was going to make a forced landing and requested that one of our VFs investigate a small island to the northeast of us and due north of the Camotes Islands, which I felt I could land near if it appeared to be friendly. I also spoke to my crew, ARM/2c R. G. Hessong, and AOM/2c R. D. Henry, who remained calm and were helpful in our successful ditching of the aircraft. However, my oil pressure soon read "zero" so I decided to land about 5 miles west of San Francisco Island of the Camotes group. My crewmen got set, the radioman climbing forward into the second cockpit where we had a safety belt rigged for such emergencies, and I decided to land near several native sailboats that were heading west toward Cebu Island, requesting that VF cover my landing. I set the aircraft down on a calm sea and we ditched her. My radioman, being the first out, he and I released and inflated our three-man life raft, while the turret gunner got clear and then rescued our emergency back-packs from the plane. Our TBM floated for about two minutes so I had an opportunity to look the plane over, and the wings and fuselage were riddled with holes and the tail surfaces were almost in shreds. There is no question in my mind but that my own frag clusters were the cause of our forced landing. We shoved off with all of our equipment in the three-man raft and we were almost immediately within hailing distance of a large native sailboat which appeared to be manned by natives. I ordered my oarsman to approach cautiously, warning them to be ready to use their .38s if the natives proved to be Japs or unfriendly natives. However, the natives immediately assured us of their friendliness by their greetings and I was able to satisfy myself further by talking with them in my 2.0 Spanish. We climbed aboard and secured our life raft and our equipment in the sailboat, where-upon they set course for San Francisco Island, from which they had come, having been on their way to trade in Cebu.

COMMANDER T. H. WINTERS, EN

I received Lt. (jg) McDonald's transmission that he was going to make a forced landing and I was able to locate him as the lowest flying aircraft in the rendezvousing strike group. Lieut. Seckle, my wingman, and I flew cover on McDonald and orbited over his aircraft after he crash-landed. I also contacted the two lifeguard submarines in the area over VHF and got a "Roger" from each. I also advised the VOS Air/Rescue people of the crash. We watched McDonald and his crewmen ditch their aircraft, inflate their life raft and paddle towards a large sailboat which was approaching them. We flew low over the sailboat to assure ourselves that it was native owned and not manned by Japs. We orbited until McDonald gave us the "Thumbs-up" signal and then we left the immediate area in order not to attract the attention of any Jap aircraft or surface vessels in the vicinity. We watched the sailboat at a distance as she set course for San Francisco Island and laid our plans for rescuing McDonald and his crewmen the following day.

LT. (JG) J. S. McDONALD, USNR

The native sailboat which rescued us had log out-riggers; the mainmast was stepped well forward; and both the main and the jib sails were made from woven matting. She had a small, low cabin aft, covered inside with bamboo mats. (This type of sailboat is common in the Visayan Islands. The Japs have taken over all power craft. A good rule of thumb for pilots is to avoid all power craft. Sailboats are usually manned by friendly natives.) The occupants, two elderly men; 2 small boys, 14 and 16; and 2 women with babies, were friendly but shy. They told us afterwards that they knew we were Americans as they had recognized the insignia on the wing of our air-craft. The natives were sculling with their oars as there was a little wind, however a light squall increased our progress near San Francisco Island. Evidently the natives on San Francisco had seen our plane crash because there were 200 to 300 natives cheering and waving when our sailboat came into a small fishing village. We were given a friendly welcome by these natives and then were taken to the largest house in the village, a two story building with a galvanized iron road, built on stilts about 30 yards from the beach, belonging to one Miguel Daffon. Daffon spoke English with difficulty, explaining that it had been some time since he had spoken English. However, we were able to understand each other quite well. Daffon took us into his house, gave us clean clothes, ordered that our flight gear be washed and hung out in the sun by his woman and had the equipment in our back-packs laid out to dry. We were given white linen trousers to wear. I got a pink "T" shirt, Hessong a blue one and Henry a yellow one. We were all dressed up with no place to go. However, Daffon gave a big dinner for us that evening, chicken, rice, corn on the cob, etc., but without any seasoning. After dinner Daffon called a meeting which included himself; Salvadore, a private in the Philippine Scouts for 16 years; and several other leading men in the village. However, there were several hundred natives present sitting outside the circle and standing in the shadows, their eyes glistening like wild animals' in the darkness. Daffon, who was a sergeant in the Philippine Army, wore his Philippine Army uniform for the occasion. After dinner he dispatched a field order concerning our arrival on San Francisco Island to be delivered by runner to the Captain of the island. I had some military experience before I became a Navy officer and I recognized the field order as being well written. After native entertainment by Daffon's son, who sang and played his guitar for us, I was able to talk with Daffon and Salvadore and to learn something of their experiences and background.

Daffon told me that he had been a sergeant in the Philippine Army stationed on Luzon when the Japanese invaded the Philippines. He states that he had fought against the Japanese until resistance was no longer possible. Daffon took his wife and 6 children together with Salvadore and his family and they worked their way south to Leyte ahead of the Japanese, hiding by day and island-hopping by night. On Leyte, Daffon and Salvadore joined the guerrilla or volunteer forces under one Major Soliman, who had been in either the Philippine Scouts or the Philippine Army on Luzon. According to Daffon, Major Soliman held the rank of Colonel in the guerrilla forces. He was captured later in a battle with the Japanese on Leyte when the guerrilla forces resisted Jap occupation with crude weapons and bolo knives in 1942. He was taken prisoner to Luzon, where he was confined but escaped shortly thereafter, according to Daffon, being assisted by the underground guerrilla forces on Luzon to escape. Daffon said that he believed Soliman had made his way to Australia and that he was with General MacArthur's forces there. After Soliman's capture, on Leyte, organized resistance to the Japs ceased according to Daffon except for occasional raids by the guerrillas on isolated islands that were weakly defended by the Japanese and where the guerrillas and their families would not be subject to reprisal from the Japanese. Two officers, one Miranda and one Konleon, who were both in the Philippine Scouts, took over the command of the guerrilla forces. However, Miranda and Konleon quarreled according to Daffon so they agreed to establish separate defense areas on Leyte. Konleon took command of the guerrilla forces in eastern Leyte and Miranda assumed command of the forces in western Leyte. The rivalry between these two Philippine guerilla leaders flared again, however, and finally resulted in civil war. Konleon attacked Miranda's forces, defeating them, taking the officers prisoner and poisoning the minds of the guerrilla soldiers against Miranda and his officers, Daffon being one of their number. However, Miranda escaped and was able to intercede for his officers with Konleon, agreeing that his forces would pledge their loyalty to Konleon and that he and his officers would retire from the guerrilla forces. Thus, Daffon and Salvadore left Leyte with their families and sailed southwest where they were apprehended by the Japanese. Daffon said that he and Salvadore pretended not to know any English and they spoke only Spanish, posing as fishermen. They were finally released and fortunately so, because their captors were on the lookout for guerrilla leaders who they said had recently fled from Leyte. After this experience Daffon and Salvadore and their families sailed to San Francisco Island, where they have resided for the past two years. Daffon stated that they are bothered only infrequently by the Japanese, usually by small patrols of 5 or 6 men from Leyte who come to commandeer the natives' food supply. He said that the natives have been passive in their resistance to these patrols as they know that they would be subject to reprisal from the large forces in Leyte. On one occasion, a native failed to give up his entire food supply, saving some grain for his family to last through the drought. The Japanese hanged him by his fingers from the limb of a tree for his trouble, his fingers, wrists, arms and shoulders being out of joint when he was taken down by the natives after the patrol had left the island. Daffon said that outside of the Japanese, their major problem was to grow or obtain enough food, especially during periods of drought. Secondly, they had no medical supplies on the island other than native remedies. Also, they had been unable to obtain any cloth for over two years and their clothing was reduced to rags. However, he said that San Francisco was healthful and that there was no malaria or other serious, contagious diseases. (McDonald and his crewmen slept here on the night of 13 September and they were not bothered by mosquitoes or other insects in Daffon's house.)

(It should be stated that Lt. (jg) McDonald did not expect to be rescued the following day, on 14 September, and that he had an opportunity to talk with his hosts only generally about the guerrilla activities and the strength of the Japanese in the Visayans.) I was interested in the guerrillas' activities in the Visayans and I soon saw that Daffon and Salvadore were proud and anxious to tell me about them. They explained that the Visayans are divided into Defense Districts, one Defense District being on Leyte and the 9th Defense District being on Cebu under a Colonel Spaulding, whose headquarters are located northwest of Cebu City, in the central mountain range on the island. He also said that many of the guerrilla forces are strongly organized on Leyte, where they have been regularly supplied by U. S. submarines. The guerrillas are well armed with U. S. weapons and are ready for the time when they can support our landings in the Visayans from the rear. They have been training their forces for the past two years in the use of U. S.

weapons and their own deadly bolo knives. According to Daffon, the guerrillas on Leyte drill twice each week, study tactics from U. S. Army Manuals
and plan for their day of liberation in their hideaways in the southern and
central mountains of Leyte. He stated that there were some Filipino pilots
and mechanics who had escaped from Luzon also on Leyte. The guerrillas
have radio facilities which they use to contact U. S. forces and possibly other
guerrilla centers in the islands. He stated that they have scouts on the alert
and couriers who carry documents and orders between the islands on duty
at all times. Leyte is also the propaganda center in the Visayans. Daffon
showed me a copy of the June, 1944 issue of the Philippine Independence, a
newspaper published by the Philippine government in the United States,
which he said was distributed from Leyte, being brought in by U. S. submarines. Daffon and Salvadore were reasonably well informed about the progress of the war, being most anxious to know when General MacArthur was
going to invade the Philippines.

I asked Daffon and Salvadore about Japanese activities in the Visayans,
but their knowledge seemed to be restricted chiefly to Leyte. They stated
that the Japanese were feverishly strengthening their positions on Leyte,
building new airfields, motor transport areas, and barracks and supply facilities. Salvadore said that the Japanese had been doing considerable night
flying in the area and that aircraft were seen frequently over the Camotes
Islands. He also mentioned that shortly after our first strike against Cebu he
had observed several flights of aircraft flying to the north toward Luzon.
Daffon stated that the Japanese have been building up Ormoc on Leyte as a
large supply base with new construction of barracks and buildings, a large
motor transport center and concentrations of enemy troops.

As to Luzon, Daffon said that he was not reliably informed about guerrilla activities on Luzon but he understood that they operated underground,
with friendly forces operating in the mountainous areas principally of the
north of Manila. I asked about Mindanao and he said that he did not have
any information except about Davao, which he understood was strongly
held by the Japanese, there being few friendly natives there.

We had crash-landed about 1530 and I was tired and Henry and Hessong
seemed to be too, it now being about 2200. I was also concerned about the
native fires attracting Jap patrols, although Daffon had told me that there

were no Japanese on the island. Daffon saw that we wanted to get some rest so he led us into the house and showed us to our bedroom. The entire family and many of their friends, women included, followed us. There were two beds, one double for Henry and Hessong and a single for me; that is, frames with board slats. I kept waiting for them to bring out the mattresses, but of course this was not the case. Daffon's wife brought out clean bedspreads for the beds and Daffon gave us some pajama pants. I thanked him for his courtesy and kindness to us and prepared to undress, thinking that everyone would leave the bedroom. However, they just stood and watched us, women too, seeming to enjoy the entire situation. I didn't know what to do in front of the native women so I told Henry and Hessong to undress down to their shorts, then wait and see what would happen. Nothing happened—nobody moved, so we put the pajamas on over our shorts and got into bed. That seemed to satisfy everyone, because they left immediately. I couldn't sleep, partly because of the beds and also because I was uneasy about the possibility of a Jap patrol moving in while we were asleep, so I decided to be a "one-man-army," got up, dressed and ran patrols up and down the beach with my .45 for several hours. However, everything seemed quiet and the natives were not uneasy so I went back to bed and had a sound sleep.

Henry and Hessong awakened me the next morning, the 14th, to advise me that the Captain of the Island had received Daffon's message and that he was waiting below to meet us. He was a fine looking Filipino about 26 years old. He was armed with a .45 pistol and his two men were armed with M-1 carbines and they wore bandoleers. The Captain told me that he was going to take me to Cebu to the headquarters of Colonel Spaulding, who would assist us in making our escape to Australia. He explained to me that we would go to Cebu by sailboat from a remote place on San Francisco and that we should be ready to leave in a short time. However, VOS aircraft from our Task Force, led and escorted by Commander Winters, flew over the island soon thereafter and effected our rescue.

A native, shortly thereafter, came to the house saying that aircraft were circling low over the beach. Hessong, Henry and I ran down to the beach to see what was happening. I had our Very pistol with me. The OS2Us were flying low over the water and almost out of sight. However, I attempted to fire the pistol at the last OS2U, but I forgot to release the safety catch and it, of course, did not fire. However, one OS2U landed on the water and I finally fired the Very pistol which the pilot saw and he taxied in toward the beach. The other OS2Us prepared to land also.

There were 200 or 300 natives on the beaches by this time, cheering and clapping their hands with excitement. Daffon and Salvadore were there too, so we took our leave of them right there. I did my best to express our appreciation for their shelter and hospitality. I had previously written a letter for Daffon officially expressing my appreciation for his kindness, for him to use when our forces landed in the Visayans. We were dressed in the clothes that Daffon had given us, but he insisted that we take them even though I am sure they were his best things. I gave Daffon my .45 pistol, shoulder holster, bolo knife, 90 rounds of ammunition and our effects. We also gave them our three-man life raft, instructing them to change the yellow colored bottom and to hide it from the Japanese. We also left our emergency back-pack kits with them, explaining how the various items should be used. Then we swam out to the OS2Us.

COMMANDER T. H. WINTERS, USN

We took off from the U.S.S. *Lexington* at 0645 on the 14th, our four VF rendezvousing with four VOS from the Task Force, two OS2Us from the U.S.S. *Indiana* and two OS2Us from the U.S.S. *Santa Fe*. We proceeded to the vicinity of the Camotes Islands where I had seen McDonald and his crewmen headed in the native sailboat the previous afternoon. We spent over an hour searching the coastline of the islands, at 50' along the beaches, flaps down in our VF, and although we passed several groups of huts and groups of cheering and clapping natives we would find no trace of the survivors. I was almost ready to depart when, in desperation, I ordered one of the OS2Us to land on the water in front of the largest group of huts on San Francisco Island and instructed the pilot to get the natives to come out to him so that he could inquire about McDonald. However, he had no sooner landed and begun to taxi in toward the beach when a Very pistol was fired from the beach and we knew that we were on the right track. After a few minutes the survivors appeared on the beach and then swam out to the OS2Us and climbed into the empty rear seat cockpits. After take-off and rendezvous, the OS2Us from the U.S.S. *Indiana* reported two and one-half hours and the OS2Us from the U.S.S. *Santa Fe* three and one-half hours of fuel left. On the 13th another pilot had been reported being down about 10 miles to the south. I ordered the OS2Us from the U.S.S. *Santa Fe* to proceed to the south and the U.S.S. *Indiana* OS2Us to return to base with VF cover. Our search for the missing pilot was unsuccessful, and due to the shortness of fuel in the OS2Us, we returned to base at 1238/I after almost 6 hours of search. One OS2U, after landing beside the U.S.S. *Santa Fe*, ran out of gas while taxiing on the water. Our VG had 60 to 70 gallons of fuel remaining.

These are some of the most important survival facts that Lt. (jg) McDonald gained from his short experience:

1. The entire Camotes Islands, particularly San Francisco Island, may be added to the list of friendly areas in the Visayan Islands. (Guerrilla Force Dispositions, 15 August 1944, map disseminated by Military Intelligence Section, General Staff, General Headquarters North West Pacific Area.)

2. There have been few instances of the natives in the Visayan Islands cooperating with the Japanese, according to his informants, and these have been in the cities and towns where they are under Japanese pressure. Although caution is advised, natives encountered will usually be friendly.

3. It is believed that pilots or air crewmen who are forced down in these islands can, in most instances, get ashore safely and without being detected by the Japanese if they make their landings away from the cities and towns and military installations.

4. Those Filipinos who have had previous military experience in the U. S. Army or the Philippine Scouts are usually the military leaders of the guerrilla or volunteer forces, and you should make every effort to contact these people. After you have placed yourself in their hands, don't be impatient about how you are going to escape from enemy territory. Allow them to make the necessary arrangements through regular military channels as their guerrilla forces are in constant and regular contact with our forces. They may attempt to have you evacuated by submarine or you may have to hide away until our forces invade the Visayan Islands. However, it is well for a pilot to explain how much more impor-

tant a job he can do if he is returned as soon as possible to his own forces.

5. Survivors should remember, especially, that the Filipinos are not only friendly to our cause but that they are a proud and patriotic people who have suffered a great deal in their resistance of Japanese aggression. You will offend them, however, if you show pity or sympathy for their situation. They regard the United States as the mother country so you should conduct yourself in line with your rank or rate in the U. S. Navy at all times.

8

---

142 SURVIVORS

The air-sea rescue machinery moved forward behind the battles and, in this story, saved 142 seamen in the ocean after their ship sank. The enormous lifting capabilities of the PBY are evident—one rescue plane took off with 56 survivors on board, and another used three miles on its takeoff run.

****

On 3 December 1944, four PBY-5s of VPB-34 flew five rescue sorties to Ormoc Bay and picked up a total of 142 survivors of a destroyer which had been sunk on the previous night. The success of this mass air-sea rescue operation is a further demonstration both of the ruggedness of the Cats and the versatility of VPB-34.

Lt. (jg) Essary took off from San Pedro Bay at 0725. Two other planes of the squadron were airborne about the same time, and the three of them immediately proceeded to the point of rendezvous with their fighter escort. However, no fighters appeared, and as bogeys had been reported in the area the rescue planes were ordered not to proceed until they had fighter cover. Seven P-47s arrived at 1135, and this was considered to be sufficient cover for only two of the rescue planes. Essary and Lt. (jg) Ball proceeded on their mission with the P-47s, leaving the third Cat to wait for additional fighters.

Upon arrival in the Ormoc Bay-Camotes Sea area, the two planes split up, with Essary taking the eastern half of the area and conducting a strip search of the Camotes Sea from north to south along the west coast of Leyte and westward to the Camotes Islands area. Shortly after he had started his search, he saw a large number of men in the water, some in life rafts, some in life nets, and some swimming.

Essary put the plane down about three miles east of Ormoc Peninsula. There was a light swell with a four-knot breeze from the east. There were sixteen survivors in a life net where the plane landed and they were all picked up. Essary then taxied a mile and a half up the bay, where twelve more men were taken aboard from a life raft. Sixteen more survivors were picked up in the general area, with the plane taxiing from one to another.

By this time there were 44 survivors in the plane, plus the crew of seven, and there were no more to be seen in the water. Essary took off, the plane becoming airborne after a two and a half minute run, and returned to base without fighter cover, landing at 1435.

Lt. (jg) Ball, who had flown out with Essary, searched the western half of the area, and at 1330 he sighted a number of survivors in rafts and float nets near the entrance to Ormoc Bay. The plane landed about two miles ESE of the southeast tip of Ormoc Peninsula. The sea was calm with only a light swell and a two or three knot breeze from ENE. The plane taxied up to the first group of survivors, and ten men in life jackets were brought aboard through the turret and gun blister. There were a number of others in the neighborhood and Ball taxied for about a mile and a half, taking aboard survivors until there was a total of thirty.

Four of these were picked up at a point about 1500 yards off the coast from the town of Merida. While making this pick-up, two well-camouflaged Jap DEs were observed anchored in close to the coast in a small cove a little to the north of Merida and about two miles from the plane. However, the rescue operations were not interrupted by gunfire, as the DEs apparently were more inclined to remain hidden than they were to fire on the Cat. Several of the survivors said that during the morning a plane which they thought to have been a P-47 dropped a bomb very close to the DEs.

At this time the fighters called the rescue plane and directed it to more survivors across the bay near the town of Albuera and about a mile off the coast. The plane taxied over and picked up 22 more survivors. They soon came upon another group of about 30 and picked up four of the most seriously wounded. By this time they had taken aboard 56 survivors in addition to the crew of seven. The most seriously injured were in bunks, and the others were packed throughout the plane from the bow gunner's position to the aft section of the fuselage. One of the survivors manned the bow .30s, partly because he had no alternative and partly because he was hoping for a crack at the Japs.

Ball called the base with advice of the position of the remaining survivors and then took off, after leaving them a seven man life raft. He had to make a run of three miles before he was airborne. On the way back he met Lt. (jg) Day and directed him to the survivors. He landed at the base at 1545 with the 56 survivors, including the commanding officer of the DD.

Lt. (jg) Day took off with the other rescue planes but was held up by the absence of fighter cover. At 1350 there was a call for additional rescue planes, and at 1400 Day got under way with an escort of four P-38s. As mentioned in the preceding paragraphs, he met Ball coming back and got his instructions. Day landed near the group that of necessity had been left behind by Ball, and taxied over to them. Most of them were clustered in a group around a life net and a large life raft. He picked up 26, all that were in sight, and then took off again to sweep the bay for more. Results of the sweep were negative, and Day detached two of the P-38s to cover Lt. (jg) Gillard, who had just arrived in another Dumbo. He then proceeded to base, dragging the coast at 50 feet as he went. The plane landed at 1648.

Lt. (jg) Gillard took off for the rescue mission at 1430 to assist in the rescue operations then in progress in Ormoc Bay. By the time that he arrived, having proceeded without fighter cover, the bay was completely cleaned of American survivors, although there were quite a few Japs floating about. First he searched the open sea area around the Camotes Islands, and then he flew in low and along the coasts of the islands.

Near a town, he noticed that people along the beach and near a concrete jetty were waving at him and apparently trying to attract his attention. He landed and taxied up to the jetty, which extended out about 100 feet from the shore. A number of Filipinos came out to the plane in canoes and reported that they had some survivors on the island.

Shortly afterwards, another PBY-5, commanded by Lt. (jg) Harrison, landed and came up nearby. The local people brought out sixteen survivors and nine of them got aboard Gillard's plane. The natives also said that they thought there were more survivors in the hills. They had apparently observed the engagement of the night before and said that they had seen the DD sink and also four or five Jap ships go down.

Lt. (jg) Harrison took off at 1530 in the same plane which had originally been flown by Essary. He was covered by four P-38s and went directly to Ormoc Bay. He searched first along the west coast of Leyte with negative results. He then started to sweep the Camotes Sea and soon observed Gillard's plane. He landed and taxied up alongside as indicated above. Seven of the sixteen survivors were put in his plane. One of the natives said that the surrounding waters had been thoroughly searched with canoes and that there were no more.

Both planes took off and, after further search with negative results, headed for base. They landed at 1800.

9

SURVIVAL STORIES OF BOMBING SEVEN

These survival narratives covering October experiences of VB-7 pilots and personnel in the Formosa-Philippines area were forwarded in a personal letter from the Squadron ACI Office. The first account is told in the first person by the pilot, Lt. (jg) Alders, as he experienced it; the others were written.

****

PART 1: SIXTEEN MEN ON A RAFT

We went in at 1530 on October 25th. The plane floated about three minutes, and the gunner and myself were able to get in our rubber boat. The first twenty-four hours passed without incident although both of us were very ill during that time. At 1115 on the 26th, an OS2U passed directly overhead, but we did not have time to get a smoke bomb out and other methods failed to attract attention. We had no food nor water until the morning of the 27th when we caught about a quart of rain water in a piece of canvas.

The middle of that afternoon, our third day, we saw a PBM flying at about 5000 feet and so far away as to be almost a speck in the distance. We broke out a smoke bomb and fortunately they saw it. After circling for an hour and a half they landed, but sprang a leak in the hull in doing so, with the result that when the plane took off all the shipped water rolled aft, threw the tail down and the nose up, and caused us to spin in from a height of about 100 feet.

Everybody aboard managed to get out OK, but not long afterward one fellow died, apparently from swallowing too much sea water, which had a strong content of gasoline from the ruptured tanks of the plane. There were no marks of injury on him and his life jacket was inflated, but he was obviously full of that mixture. He was buried at sea with a prayer.

One seven-man life raft containing no food or water was salvaged from the PBM. There were sixteen of us, and after some experiments we found that with two-men in the water, the other fourteen could get support from the raft although it did not float above the surface. The two-man shift in the water was rotated every fifteen minutes.

Around 1800 we found ourselves being followed by a shark about six feet in length. He would circle and glide in towards the men in the water, then as soon as he would get within oar's length, we would beat him off. One time he stuck his nose out of water and received a sound smack right in the puss. That time he left in a hurry, but came back in about an hour with two others. They stayed with us until we were rescued, often swimming within a few feet of the raft, but never made a determined attack on the boys in the water—probably because the rest of us kept busy with the oars.

At 0915 on October 28th a Jap Tony flew over at 3000 feet but evidently did not see us. Then at 1030 we saw four SB2Cs. There was a Very pistol in the raft, and with it we attracted their attention. A destroyer was sent from the fleet one hundred and fifty miles away, and picked us up. Even then the excitement was not quite over because an hour later a sub fired a torpedo at us, but missed.

I believe the most important thing that was learned on the raft was that a smoke bomb seems to be the most effective means of attracting attention. The gunner and I experienced no desire for food or water the first two days but that may have been because we were so ill. It is worth noting that after four days' immersion, our .38 pistols, although very rusty, would still fire. An occasional shot seems to keep rust out of the barrel. Incidentally tracer bullets are very easy to see, day or night, and then provision of tracer ammunition would seem to be very important. It was the means of saving one of the fighter pilots of our squadron.

PART 2: PILOT MAKES BASE ON AMMONIA

Lieut. Lutey of VB-7 was participating in an attack on a Formosa target on 12 October. Just after releasing his wing bombs in a second run over the target, his plane and himself were hit by AA fire, probably 40 mm. In his own words, "I heard considerable racket and observed that blood was pouring through a hole in my left trouser leg midway between ankle and knee. I stuck my hand in the hole to slow down the flow until I was clear of the target area."

The Group Medical Officer had issued to all pilots a first aid kit which contained a tourniquet, but Lutey had removed the tourniquet and stowed it in his belt. There it had worked around to the back under his holster, where he couldn't pry it out with one hand. He took a compress from the kit and applied that.

Meanwhile the cockpit floor was awash with mixed blood and hydraulic fluid and he was about to lose consciousness, so he opened one of the four ammonia ampoules in the kit and sniffed it. These ampoules undoubtedly saved his life and should be a standard item of equipment. He sniffed three of them until they were used up, and drank the fourth when he was afraid it wouldn't last. He says as a drink it is inferior and tastes like bad bootleg gin. There definitely, he thought, should be water to chase it with—which at the moment there wasn't.

In the meantime, whenever his plane was observed to waver or change direction, the flight leader called him on the radio, giving him instructions and encouragement. This was extremely helpful, he reported, and is recommended in similar circumstance.

He reached the destroyer screen and made a no-flap landing. Through the strenuous and effective efforts of his gunner he was gotten into the raft, and shortly they were both picked up.

PART 3: LIGHTED RAFT SAVES PILOT

On 29 October, after a strike against cruisers in Manila Bay, the flight returned at dusk to find the task group in the middle of a rain squall. It became dark soon thereafter and everyone was low on gas. Of the six planes we had in the flight, one, badly shot up, crashed on the deck and was thrown overboard. Three made water landings, one landed on the Intrepid.

Lt. (jg) Edmonds, of VB-7, was the sixth and also landed on the Intrepid but hit the catwalk on the starboard side and flopped over on his back. He saw a flash of fire and, thinking the plane would flare up, unfastened his safety belt and dropped upside down into the sea. His gunner was hauled out of the plane with minor injuries. The next thing Edmonds remembers was fighting his way to the surface. His gun with tracer ammunition and his waterproof light had both been ripped off and he would have been lost almost certainly, but the Intrepid threw over a life raft which had (1) a light attached which was lighted, so he could find it and the destroyer could find him, and (2) a sea anchor, making it possible for him to swim to the raft before it drifted away.

This equipment should be mandatory on every carrier.

It should also be noted that it is much easier to climb into a life raft by taking your Mae West off first and stowing it inside.

PART 4: PHILIPPINE NATIVES HOSPITABLE TO GUNNER

J. Trapp, ARM2c, was gunner for Lt. (JG) Robertson. In the attack on the Jap fleet units off Samar, his plane was hit at the beginning of the pull-out. The right wing caught fire, which Robertson put out by side-slipping at 200 feet over a heavy cruiser and two destroyers, but the fire started again on join-up and he made a crash water landing.

Trapp got out and into the raft but Robertson sank before Trapp could get to him and didn't come up again. A short time later the whole Jap fleet came through and the DDs passed within 50 feet. Jap sailors yelled at him and shook their fists but apparently no one shot at him. Trapp was exhausted and tied himself in the raft and went to sleep.

He woke up in a storm in the middle of the night, caught some water in the sheet and drank it; he also threw out the sea anchor. To keep warm he put some sea water in the raft and covered himself with the poncho. (Water is warmer than the air at night but this practice is not recommended if you're going to be in the raft for more than three or four days.)

Next morning he set sail to westward with good wind and sighted mountains in the afternoon. When the wind died he started to row, but saw large breakers in the offing so he stopped and decided to wait until morning, and put his sea anchor out again. The next afternoon, after much rowing on a hot windless day, he reached the reef, which had twelve-foot breakers without apparent entrance. The first time he tried to get in by swimming away from the raft and was unsuccessful, as the undertow pulled him out; the next time he held onto the raft and was successful.

He waded ashore and found a native hut. The inhabitants of the hut couldn't speak English and were very poor, but understood he was an American and gave him food, which tasted like turnips and sweet potatoes, in a coconut shell; and water, which was very bad. (After that he used coconuts exclusively for drinking.) Shortly a native who spoke English came along and took him to a village on the coast.

All the inhabitants were very friendly and delighted to hear that the Americans were coming; they immediately started to celebrate. He was then bundled into a boat and paddled to a larger island where he was met by a group of the local guerrillas, word having been passed somehow by the grapevine. He was taken to the guerrilla leader, and met numerous other guerrillas; all of them were very confident and said that with enough arms, ammunition and cigarettes (American cigarettes were selling for ten cents apiece) they would kill all the Japs themselves.

The next day a party, which included the guerrilla chief and Trapp, got aboard an ancient launch and headed down the coast. They were in danger of attack by both Japanese and Americans, and a PBY broke off a run on them only after frantic use of the blinker. At one stop they picked up a survivor from a DD which had been sunk by the Jap fleet CVEs.

They traveled in the daytime, and each night they went ashore and the villagers threw a party. Finally they were picked up by an LCI and transferred to a Liberty ship, and from there to a DD. Trapp was put ashore at Hollandia and managed to get back to the ship a few days later, in spite of constant attempts made at each advanced base to put him on working parties and ignore his request for transportation.

Note: The most noteworthy thing about this story is the almost unanimous friendly feeling displayed by the Filipinos. With the exception of a few spies and opportunists they all will help and assist downed fliers in every way possible. It is also felt that Trapp showed a great deal of ingenuity and resourcefulness in getting himself out of what might have been a very tough spot.

PART 5: DUNKED THREE TIMES IN THREE DAYS

The following story is based on an interview with Lt. (jg) W.J. Ennis, who would have seemed to hold the squadron record of VB-7 for immersion, having ended up in the water on three occasions in four successive days of flying. In the first two cases, enemy AA was the contributing factor; in the third—as a passenger—Ennis went into the water because of weather.

The first water-landing took place on 26 October. Ennis and his squadron took off to attack the retreating Japanese fleet. They found and attacked a heavy cruiser. Ennis was the third man to dive. At 5000-6000 feet, his aircraft was hit in the left wing by AA. He continued his dive and released his bomb at 1500 feet. Shortly after the release, his plane was hit again by automatic weapons.

Upon retirement he found that the SB2C needed 20 degrees right rudder and 20 degrees of right wing depression to fly. He was obliged to put both feet on the rudder and hold the stick in the extreme right hand position. In this situation he retired across the enemy-held islands at about 2000 feet. He was unable to climb and the AA had knocked out his compass and airspeed indicator.

He managed to get within 15 miles of the task force and then ran out of gas. In spite of the damaged condition of the plane, he made a successful dead-stick water landing and he and his gunner got out safely and inflated their rubber raft. Planes circling above them directed a destroyer to the raft, and they were picked up 40 minutes after landing. (Regarding his experiences with the raft, Ennis suggests that, rather than throw out dye markers in a package, the markers be tied to the side of the raft so that even though the raft may drift fast, your position will continue to be spotted.)

On 29 October, Ennis took part in the shipping strike at Manila Bay. In his second dive, he released his bomb at 1800 feet and was hit by AA but did not realize it until he saw oil pressure dropping and his engine started to run roughly. Employing full throttle, he managed to regain his position in formation and signaled that he was in trouble. The oil pressure continued to drop and the engine gradually lost power until he was forced to make a water landing.

Again he and his gunner, Meredith, successfully escaped from the plane and got out the raft. TBMs dropped back packs but Ennis was able to retrieve only one of them. The water was quite choppy and progress in the raft was difficult. F6Fs orbited the raft until two Kingfishers landed and took Ennis and Meredith aboard. Two F6Fs escorted them toward base. By radio they heard that their ship was under attack and were warned to be on the lookout for enemy aircraft.

At 1800 they encountered a heavy equatorial front and tried without success to fly around the storm area.

Ennis:

"At 1845, it was getting dark and we found out that the force was in the middle of this bad weather. We force-landed at about 1850 while it was still faintly light. The other OS2U landed close by but we soon lost sight of them in the rough water. It was raining very hard at this time. One of our fighter escorts was running low on gas and he too decided to put it down. We had all our lights on, trying to get him as close to us as possible. Evidently he lost sight of us, as he landed about a half a mile behind us, appearing to hit very hard. We tried to turn around to see if we could be of help but we almost capsized in the choppy water. We had to stay directly into the wind. We taxied, as we would never be able to keep the plane afloat otherwise in the rough water, and that was 100 per cent better than to get into a life raft again —to say nothing of the fact there were three of us for a two man raft.

"About an hour after we had landed, two F6Fs came close by. One came very low—firing a short burst. Naturally we were startled. I didn't know whether it was a signal but we turned off all our lights immediately.

"Time went on. One rain squall ran into another. I fired Very stars steadily and kept my flash-light on. The visibility for the most part was practically nil and that cut down our chances of being picked up. At about midnight the weather started to clear and a pretty good-sized moon became visible. The wind died down and the seas calmed down considerably.

"At approximately 0130 I fired two Very stars half-heartedly, as I thought I saw ships out in darkness. I thought to myself that it just couldn't be. All I could think of was that the force had been under attack and that they had probably left the area in nothing flat. I couldn't see why they would stay around. They wouldn't be looking for a few pilots at the risk of the whole task force.

"The next thing we knew, a destroyer was bearing down on us; it looked as if he would cut us in two for a while there.

"None of us recognized the ship. It looked too big for a destroyer yet it was much too small for a cruiser. Then there were two of them on the scene. One on the upwind side of us, the other on the down-wing side. Then we could see in the distance what looked like a battleship closing in. Shortly after that a blinker was being sent from one ship to another. About that time we were convinced that they were Jap ships and decided to ditch the plane, as it was about to run out of gas. We figured they would follow the plane and forget about its passengers. We all slid off the starboard wing into the water —bringing the raft with us. The plane went on its merry way.

"One of the ships got very close to us in the raft at this time and put an amber search light on us. That light was replaced shortly by a white one. Then we could hear American voices. Believe me, we were three happy young men! We were pulled aboard at about 0245 and given a hot shower and dry clothes.

"Returned to own ship the next morning."

10

DUMBO TAKES A HIT

The following third-person report was filed on behalf of the crewmen involved.

****

The PBM was headed for the drink. She had skimmed over New Ireland, bombing and strafing for the last time. Hit in six places by AA and afire in one engine, she was losing power like a punctured balloon. Her hydraulic system was shot out, her wheels dangled from the nacelles, and her port stabilizer had a hole big enough to drop a football through.

The skipper knew from the look of things that they were going to get wet. With him were six other men: co-pilot, navigator-bombardier, radioman, turret gunner, tail gunner, and cameraman. They took ditching positions and the pilot led the bomber by the hand and set her down in an excellent water landing about two and a half miles from Cape Namaroda, New Guinea. No one was injured; everyone got out successfully and climbed aboard the large emergency raft.

Always alert for a sporting setup of this kind, the enemy shore positions took the raft under fire with automatic weapons, machine guns, and three-inch shells. The fire continued, with occasional interruptions, for approximately two hours. The volume was fairly intense at times and the water near the raft was peppered with slugs. Several holes were punctured in the raft and one piece of shrapnel struck the index finger of the tail gunner, Sgt.

Harris. In order to make a smaller target, the men got out of the raft and clung to the sides. To make enemy sighting more difficult they covered the raft with blue sail cloth.

During this time three planes of VMB-4 covered the raft and strafed the gun positions. The strafing was considered fairly accurate but it silenced the guns only temporarily. It did, however, divert fire from the raft to the attacking planes, one of which suffered .303 hits that severed the gas line and forced the aircraft to depart for Green Island. This plane, piloted by Capt. Lemke, left the area at 1515 and proceeded to Green on one engine, arriving at 1605. Only one orbiting plane, that of Maj. Pritchard, was left above the raft.

Shortly after this a Dumbo was sent out to attempt a landing. The water was considered too rough, and the Dumbo merely relieved Pritchard, who was short on gas. Meanwhile, two more squadron mates of the downed fliers took off to bring help. Lt. Martin, who had returned to Green and gassed up, reappeared on the scene at 1600 and dropped the men a small life raft and some food and water bags. While circling the raft, Martin's plane drew intense shore fire.

At 1630 Lt. Col. Anderson turned up and stayed for six hours and twenty minutes. Because of rough water, it was finally decided that no landing should be attempted, but instead a PT boat would attempt the rescue. The Dumbo departed. At 1700 a PT left Green and at 1830 a PBY-5A took off to cooperate with the surface craft. Martin left the area at 1844.

The PT made the trip against heavy seas in four and a half hours. Its operations were directed by the PBY-5A and by Lt. Col. Anderson. Because of the roughness of the sea and the difficulty in establishing communications, rescue was not effected until 2250. Anderson left the area as soon as the men were aboard the PT and arrived at Green at 2315, having sustained one .303 hit from the shore fire.

The PT reached Green with its seven passengers at 0045 the next morning and they were immediately placed in the charge of the flight surgeon. Apart from the wound of Sgt. Harris, the men were uninjured and were suffering only from exhaustion due to the nervous strain and their long period in the water.

11

SKIMMING THE WAVES

The following third-person report was filed on behalf of the crewman involved.

****

Nineteen F4Us of VMF-113 and VMF-22, based at Engebi, bombed Ponape on 4 December. The weather was distinctly poor, with 7-8/10 clouds at 1,000 feet and frequent squalls. Nevertheless, the Marine fighter-bombers got in, dropped their load on target, and headed for home. It looked like a typical Marshalls strike—good results and no losses.

Then, just east of the reef, one Corsair ran into trouble, losing its engine. The pilot, 2nd Lt. Wagner of VMF-22, doesn't know whether it was the result of AA fire, an exploding ammunition dump, or simple mechanical failure. With 800 feet altitude, he had time only to point his nose down, drop flaps, and trim for a crash landing at sea. He made it very nicely, stalling out on the crest of a swell. As the F4U sank, he jumped clear. He managed to take his one-man raft with him, but his water-filled canteen tangled with the parachute harness, and he left it behind.

The raft inflated as advertised. Wagner covered himself with the tarpaulin and awaited rescue. A PBM-3D from VPH-19 circled overhead between 500 and 1,000 feet, and occasionally could be seen where the soup thinned out. Wagner floated only six miles east of the reef, to windward, but he counted on the strong southwest current to keep him clear of the island.

The time was approximately 1100, allowing plenty of daylight in which to pick him up. But there was wind of 20-25 knots, from 080°. This had two distinct disadvantages: (1) it more than off-set the current, driving the raft almost directly toward the reef, and (2) it whipped up 20 foot swells, which ordinarily would have made a seaplane landing out of the question.

For four hours the Marine pilot paddled as stoutly as he could, while Lt. Rees, in the PBM, kept his man in sight and radioed to base. A relief Dumbo and a DE were dispatched, one to arrive at 1800 that evening, the other at 0800 next morning. Rees dropped a four-man raft upwind, and the Marine got to it, trying the two rafts together.

About 1500, Wagner lay within two miles of the reef and from enemy gun positions, not to mention smaller stuff. Far from abating, the wind and weather grew worse; the only favorable feature was that this may have prevented enemy observation.

Up in the Mariner, Rees had to make a painful decision—whether to let Wagner drift to the reef and into the lagoon, where he certainly would have become a POW, or to attempt a landing in the open sea with, at a conservative estimate, 22 knots of wind. If they survived the landing, the four officers and six crewmen in the PBM stood a good chance of being POWs too. And of course there were always the big guns and smaller arms. The PBM had been stripped of its eight .50s, according to doctrine; it was a sitting duck.

Rees decided to try it anyway. The hardest part was to make an approach from far enough inland so that he could land down-wind from Wagner, who would then drift toward the plane. The area was not completely closed in; flying on instruments, watching out for the not inconsiderable land elevations on Ponape, and keeping Wagner in sight, Rees had his hands full.

He made three approaches—one crosswind, "just to make sure it couldn't be done," and then the final one. He let down over the gun positions, broke through, overshot the back of a swell he was aiming for, bounced once sixty feet, bounced again not quite so high, and came to a shuddering stop three hundred yards upwind from Wagner. The Marine pilot thought the plane had sunk until it rode up again from between two swells.

The larger raft drifted two feet, so Wagner transferred himself to the smaller one, casting the other loose. With engines cut, the PBM sailed back to Wagner, now only one and a half miles off the reef. Carefully endeavoring not to run over his man, Rees threw out a line and the Marine clambered aboard.

They prepared to get out of there, but the port engine refused to respond. For fifteen painful minutes it would not start; the eleven riders expected to draw enemy fire any second, but they remained unobserved, and the reluctant engine caught at last. The get-away was still difficult, because when Rees gave the props 1,000 rpms they churned up the swells and threatened to fall off; any thought of take-off would have been fantastic. The only way the pilot could progress at all was to rev up when approaching a swell, then chop the throttles when the plane reached the top, quaking in every plate. This process continued into the night, until they arrived at a position about 25 miles northeast of the island.

The relief Dumbo appeared, and in turn was relieved, but nothing could be done until the DE showed up. All night, as one heavy squall succeeded another, the PBM was pounded by swell after swell. How the bow window kept from collapsing, or how the wingtip floats stayed on, the pilot will never be able to explain. All night the crew stood by to abandon ship.

At 0650 next morning the DE arrived on station to find the PBM apparently none the worse from wear. The sea was still so rough the skipper hesitated about lowering a boat; it looked like throwing another helpless crew to the water. They shot a line and waited. At 0730 his mind was made up for him; after fifteen hours of as rough a pounding, probably, as any seaplane has survived, the Mariner lost its port float. Rees sent two men out on the starboard wing to keep the plane right-side up, while the rest of the crew disembarked in rafts. By skillful maneuvering, the DE launched a motor whaleboat, and picked up and transferred them uninjured to the ship. Even the boat was saved. The PBM, though, turned over on its back and was sunk by gunfire to prevent possible capture.

EPILOGUE

These stories exemplify the best of human nature. Despite being safe and comfortable in their own planes, pilots circled downed airmen for hours while others landed in high seas, putting themselves at great risk in order to help another man. But how does one walk away from someone in trouble? The answer is, you can't, and they didn't.

With gull wings, twin tails, and two engines, the Mariner's silhouette was easily recognized by any downed aviator. The PBM proved to be one of the toughest of the Pacific seaplanes. Empty, it weighed 36,000 pounds and could take on 20,000 pounds of crew, fuel, and, in these stories, survivors. Skimming atop one wave crest after the other, one pilot worked his plane 25 miles out to sea despite props that dangerously buried themselves in one wave after another. The Mariner had five watertight compartments, so sinking her took some doing, but once she broke up, she sank quickly.

12

ELEVEN DAYS IN A ONE-MAN RAFT

Lieutenant Commander Robert Price, Commander of Air Group Twenty-five, was shot down on 12 June while on a strike against an enemy convoy off the Marianas. In the following account he describes the ditching and 11 days' existence in a one-man raft.

****

"The first indication of any trouble was the sound of a metallic impact in the engine during a strafing run on an A/F. I immediately pulled up and began to smell engine oil. About 30 seconds afterwards my propeller governor failed to function and, approximately 30 more seconds after noticing this, oil pressure began to drop. The engine froze shortly after this and I began to focus my attention on a landing, after having broadcast my difficulty. It became apparent at this time that I would be forced to land almost within the convoy.

"I opened and locked the hood, got completely out of the parachute harness and tightened and locked the safety belts and shoulder straps. With flaps down, I made what seemed to be a rather hard landing into the wind, but about 20° out of the moderate sea that was running. The safety belt held me tight in the seat, however, and I was conscious only of a large quantity of water coming into the left side of the cockpit as I hit. Apparently, this was due to striking the right wing on a wave top as I hit, causing me to slew around to the right. I immediately released the safety belt and climbed out of the cockpit, attempting to pull my parachute, back pack and life raft with me. The water was already beginning to pour into the cockpit at this time, and, although I made an effort, even after the plane was completely submerged, I was unable to remove this gear. Finally, I was forced to abandon these attempts, came to the surface and pulled the life jacket toggles. The sea was rougher than I had previously estimated from the air. Each wave knocked my goggles down into my face, so I jettisoned both helmet and goggles. The belly tank, which was almost empty at this time, had ripped off and was floating about 50 feet away. I swam to it, pulling one life jacket dye marker as I did so. All this time and up until about 20 minutes after landing I could see and hear the planes of the group continuing their attack on the convoy. At the end of this time, firing ceased and the planes disappeared. I attempted to keep track of the ships in the convoy, but found this impossible because of the roughness of the water. I found I could see on occasion as far as 200-300 yards, but not further. About 15 minutes later, I saw a new type Japanese DD streaming toward me and about 200 yards away. Assuming it was searching for me, I could think of nothing better to do than to attempt to hide behind the bell tank. It came up to approximately within 75 yards, but instead of continuing towards me, it veered off and shortly disappeared. That was the last ship I saw until the day I was picked up. While hiding behind the belly tank, I caught glimpses of personnel on the destroyer lined up along the life line and bridge structure and noticed that they were wearing white shorts. I was unable to determine whether or not I had been observed, but feel that had I been I most certainly would have been picked up.

"I then attempted to settle down and get myself as comfortable as possible for what I knew was going to be a long wait. It was difficult to hang on to the belly tank, as it was bouncing around considerably, and although I had retained my gloves, the seam of the tank was cutting into my fingers. I felt some concern of being spotted subsequently from the air, but determined to make the best out of my one remaining sea marker and .45 cal. tracer ammunition, of which I had five rounds. The next five hours were spent in keeping as much water out of my face as possible. This was accomplished by heading into the sea and pulling myself up high on the tank at the crest of each wave. After about two hours, I began to notice that the tank was taking on water and not providing very much extra buoyancy. In addition, gasoline began to burn my forearms. Finally, I was forced to abandon the tank and found it more comfortable just being supported in the life jacket. Again I found the most comfortable position to be one facing into the waves and swimming over the tops of each one. This minimized the amount of water that I got in my face and eyes. The life jacket had a tendency to creep up high on my chest due to loose adjustments of the crotch strop. This forced me to float even lower in the water and necessitated constant adjustment.

"I had landed at 1100. At approximately 1600 I saw 4 F6Fs approaching and immediately pulled my one remaining dye marker and fired the .45 tracer in their direction. One plane sighted me and they all began circling. After several passes one plane dropped an unidentified object about 50 yards upwind from me. As I started to swim toward it another plane made a pass and dropped a seat type raft in the case, which landed not more than 50 feet away. I made for this instead, opened it and climbed in without difficulty. I was extremely tired by this time and experienced intense relief to be in the raft. There was a note from the pilot, saying that a seaplane would be sent out in the morning. I secured all the gear in the raft, bailed it out and put out the sea anchor. The planes left shortly and I settled down for what I assumed to be an overnight stay.

"The night passed uneventfully except for being somewhat uncomfortable due to being constantly wet and cold and having to bail out the raft at about hourly intervals. The wind was estimated to be about 12 to 15 knots in a westerly direction and occasionally white caps would break into the raft, filling it about half way. It was surprising to note that there was no tendency for it to capsize. The sea anchor carried away during the night so at daybreak I partially inflated my life jacket and found that this made a good substitute. From daybreak on I watched constantly for searching planes. These finally appeared at about 1030. Two F6Fs and an OS2U came into view quite suddenly, at which time I emptied about 2/3 of a can of sea marker and made ready to fire the last two rounds of tracer ammunition. The planes were flying at about 800 feet and were apparently at the end of their search leg as all three made a 180° turn almost over the top of me and soon disappeared in the direction from which they came. I knew now that the chances of being picked up would be slim and my morale was at a very low ebb.

"At about 1500 I saw an SB2C and an F6F apparently on a routine reconnaissance mission. They were about 10 miles away at 6 to 8 thousand feet. These were the last planes I saw until rescued. Then began a series of comparatively uneventful days and nights. I had felt no great desire for food or water and was not greatly concerned, as fish and gulls were abundant. Although rain squalls were around me almost constantly, it rained hardly at all.

"14 June—In order to minimize sunburn, I kept covered up with the sailcloth as much of the time as possible. It was difficult not to have a gap between the top of my shoes and bottom of flying suit, so I took the compress bandages out of the first aid kit (supplied in the raft) and wrapped my ankles with them. In the beginning I was uncomfortable, sitting in water constantly, but subsequently got more or less used to it. The wind was drifting me directly west in the daytime, shifting slightly toward a northerly direction in the evenings. I decided against the use of the sea anchor (life jacket) at this time, so I hauled it in and inflated it fully and used it as an improvised mattress for the bottom of the raft. This allowed me to be more comfortable for it kept buttocks and lower back out of the water. I became quite thirsty in the afternoon, but hesitated in opening the emergency can of water because large rain clouds were building up to the eastward. These broke up, however, before reaching me, and it rained within a half mile on either side of me as they separated and passed. Finally I decided on a routine of one mouthful of water from the emergency can at sunset each evening if there had been no rain during the day or night previous. I still was not hungry and spent a routine night of bailing out the raft and attempting to keep warm."

15 June—During the day I estimated the drift to be about two knots on course 280° and 285°. Without a sea anchor the raft tended to drift crosswise to the direction of the wind. Sea gulls were very abundant and tame and unhesitatingly perched on me and the end of the raft. I still didn't feel particularly hungry but decided to attempt to eat a gull to keep from

becoming so. I caught one easily by grabbing him across the back, cut off his head with my jungle knife, and skinned and cleaned him without much trouble. I attempted to eat various parts, but all were very unpalatable, being extremely salty and fishy. It seemed to make me more thirsty so I threw it overboard. In the evening the rain squalls were all around me but none passed through my area so I took a sip of water and settled down for the night.

16 June—This day was spent largely in attempting to improvise and use fishing tackle. Small schools of 4 to 6 inch perch-like fish stayed in the shade of the raft all day long and I made rather a poor hook out of the morphine styrette plug from the first aid kit. A line was made by unraveling a portion of the sea anchor line. I used all kinds of bait, including various parts of a sea gull, bits of colored cloth I could find, and inch or inch and half flying fish who, each night, somehow found their way into the bottom of the raft. All these efforts were in vain, however, as the fish would have nothing to do with my tackle.

I never saw more than 1 shark at a time, but at least one was around almost continually, feeding on the fish that lay under the raft. None of the sharks exceeded 4 or 5 feet in length and they caused no trouble. Occasionally they would cruise under the raft to scare the small fish out where they could feed on them.

The .45 automatic which I carried was in surprisingly good shape. I kept it in the holster and lashed it into the bottom of the raft where it was almost constantly submerged. As we proved later, oxidation was retarded to a great extent by doing so. At the end of the 11 days the barrel was pitted considerably but otherwise the gun was in good firing order.

I still wasn't particularly hungry, but was uncomfortably thirsty at all times, although not seriously so.

17 June—Nothing occurred this day to distinguish it from any other. It was annoying, as well as very disheartening, to see sizeable rain clouds build up in the mornings and evenings and yet never rain a drop on me. Occasionally there would be several heavy squalls all within a half mile. I tried to rig a sail at various times, but was unsuccessful. The raft was still in perfect shape. The only attention it required was to blow it up tight in the cool of the eve-

nings and relieve the pressure as the air began to expand when the sun became warm in the mornings.

18 June—I recall the nights as getting much colder, making it more difficult to sleep. This was probably due to my weakened physical condition rather than an actual change in temperature. I felt in good shape although I could see that I was losing weight. It was particularly apparent in my legs which were getting extremely small. I tried exercising them but it was difficult due to instability of the raft. A small abrasion appeared on my right elbow. I wore Marine field shoes which I never removed the whole time. Except for a slight swelling which made the shoes tight, my feet never bothered me and were in good shape when the shoes were removed. Even with the bandages around my ankles, I could tell they were getting sunburned, so I removed the bandages and coated my ankles well with boric acid ointment which is provided in the first aid kit. This seemed to help a lot and I replaced the bandages and was troubled no more. This same ointment gave adequate protection also to my face and back of hands. The fact that I stayed under the sail cloth all during the day except when bailing no doubt prevented any serious sunburn. I recall an attempt to analyze my mental condition about this time and found it surprisingly good. This, I believe, was due to two things: (1) an intense desire to live, and (2) the knowledge that every effort would be make to pick me up.

19 June—Toward evening I was lying under the sail cloth dozing when I became conscious of a commotion in the water close aboard the raft. Before I had a chance to get the sail off and look around, there were two fish practically in my arms. One was about 6 inches, and the other about 4, resembling small bass. I immediately cleaned and ate both, finding them very tasty and refreshing. They were quite juicy and helped alleviate my thirst to a great extent. Apparently they had been scared out of the water by one of the sharks making a pass under the raft for a meal.

20 June—I began to feel some concern over having had no bowel movement, but felt no desire. I urinated twice a day about a half pint each time. This surprised me at the time, inasmuch as my liquid intake was the evening swig of water of about an ounce.

21 June—This was a routine day. Most of it was spent in trying to recall the date. Up until the day I tried luck at fishing, I decided on a routine of

tying knots in a whistle lanyard for each day. However, I untied them to make fishing line and make no further attempts at date-keeping except in my head. I lost a day in calculations because when picked up I thought it was the 22nd, when actually it was the 23rd.

22 June—Nothing unusual happened on this day except that I finished the last of the emergency water at sunset. I was becoming somewhat alarmed at the total absence of rainfall, but felt that at least the law of averages should give me some rain shortly as showers were around me invariably each morning and evening. I still felt no great desire for food and was surprised at the relative amount of strength I retained. It appeared to me at this time that I had lost about 25 pounds. My legs were extremely thin.

23 June—This was the day of rescue. I began to notice effects of dehydration for the first time. This may have been due to a mental condition more than anything else because of having used all of the water the night before. At any rate, the inside of my mouth and tongue were very dry and covered with a salty scale and my tongue felt slightly swollen and prickly. At about 1645 I was sitting on the gunwales, bailing out the raft, when out of the corner of my eye I caught sight of something approaching directly from behind. I was quite startled because it took me completely by surprise. It was a destroyer approaching at a distance estimated to be about 300 yards. I couldn't identify its nationality, but could see that it had Arabic numerals painted on the bow and, of course, hoped fervently that it was one of ours. When it was about 75 yards off I heard one of the most beautiful sounds I had heard in many a day. It was, "Can you take a heaving?" I waved affirmatively, caught the line and drew myself and raft alongside the cargo net and was helped aboard by three husky bluejackets who had climbed down to give me a hand. I arrived aboard the USS *Boyd* at approximately 1700, 23 June 1944. I couldn't walk, but outside of that seemed to possess a fair amount of strength. My clothing was removed and I was stretched out on the wardroom transom. The Medical Officer looked me over and allowed a half glass of water at intervals which seemed too long. He also fed me a small cup of soup but water was the big attraction. The relief and gratification felt after having been rescued was almost indescribable and I immediately began to feel better physically. The *Boyd* came alongside the USS *Hornet* at about 1830 at which time I was transferred by stretcher and taken to the

sick bay. During the 11 days I had lost 28 pounds, but regained strength rapidly and on 6 July rejoined my Air Group.

EPILOGUE

"An intense desire to live."

"Rejoined my Air Group."

The simplicity of this story and the humble telling of an extreme experience add to the power of this narrative. Soldiers stayed stayed in the war even after enduring such extremes.

SECRET

WG-65-SJ-RE
Reel 2206

FIGHTER PILOT RESCUE FROM ENEMY TERRITORY

On 29 Dec. 1944, the Air Jungle Rescue Detachment,
10th Air Force, rescued a fighter pilot 12 miles
of Lashio. The pilot had bailed out there on 28
Dec following engine failure. The technique used by
the Rescue Detachment entailed certain risks and involved a flight requiring courage and skill. Speed
was essential, and the flight leader's compliance with
Air Force SOP on Rescue was one of the deciding factors
in this successful rescue.

The flight leader stayed with the pilot until the bail-out and noted his position
with the care required to relocate the position. He immediately notified the
Air Jungle Rescue Detachment through Fighter Control.

Air Jungle Rescue Detachment then took the following action:

(a) It dispatched a B-25 to the Fighter Squadron's home base.

(b) There it met the returning flight leader and took him on an immediate
search mission - whose purpose was to establish the position of the imperiled
pilot, drop him a para-pack containing food and other equipment and give him
initial instructions.

(c) The pilot, fortunately, was quickly located, received a pack including
a signal mirror, and was instructed to remain in hiding.

(d) During the evening the following preparations were made:

1. An early morning mission by a rescue B-25 was planned to determine
that the pilot was still in the same location and alone or with friendly
natives.

2. An L-1 was ordered to a forward base to stand by for a flight to
the open paddy where the pilot had last been seen.

3. Arrangements were made with Detachment 101, OSS to have a native
parachutist available for an alternate flight mission. If a landing
by light plane was deemed inadvisable, the parachutist would be dropped
at night to lead the pilot out on the ground.

4. A C-47 was directed to stand by at the Air Jungle Rescue Detachment
base to fly the night mission, if necessary.

5. Passengers on the B-25 morning mission would be the L-1 pilot, to
personally look at the paddy and decide whether a landing was feasible
and a representative of Detachment 101, to survey the area and determine
whether the dropping of a parachutist was advisable.

(e) The morning mission was run; the pilot located at the same point,
apparently with friendly natives; decision was made to attempt an air rescue.

A hand-typed page from the narrative section of an air-sea rescue report.

A wounded pilot is pulled aboard a PBY.

The crew assembles around a life raft dragged on to the wing of this B-25 that ditched near a Pacific island.

This P-51 pilot was escorting a formation of B-29s when he was forced to ditch. Thankfully, a Lifeguard Submarine was nearby.

After a lengthy mission over Japan, a formation of B-29s arrives home. Seen on final approach to the runways on Tinian.

SB2Cs peel out of formation to line up for their landings on the USS
Hancock, seen at the bottom of this photo.

Four crewmen crowd their rafts. Note the sail. Seen as they were found at sea.

A Dumbo taxis towards four survivors who have crowded into a single raft. Seen from under the wing of a Catalina.

Note the hills surrounding this Japanese harbor. Pilots were at risk from shells fired by the ships but also from the shore. This A-20 Havoc was hit point blank and is going down. Rescues inside these harbors were practically impossible.

The wreckage of a shapeless aircraft lies upside down next to the edge of an island thick with jungle vegetation. Survivors faced daunting prospects coming ashore against something like this.

Navy pilots like these were the men who flew and fought our war -- and in many cases were forced to ditch and suffer extreme deprivations.

Douglas SBD Dauntless dive bombers sweep across a cluster of Pacific islands. This is what these islands looked like from the altitude of search planes. Many survivors reported that planes flew over them but didn't see them. Little wonder. This photograph was taken from about 3,000 feet.

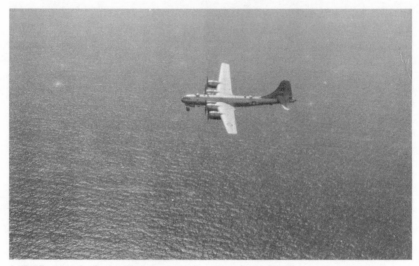

A B-29 extends its landing gear as it comes in to land.

An Australian coastwatcher. The survivors referred to the local inhabitants as "natives" and often used crude English or hand signals to communicate. The aviators were as much of a puzzle to the "natives" as the locals were to the pilots.

Smoke rises from burning Japanese tankers and supply ships.

Marine fighter pilots look at the assignments before taking off from
Henderson Field on Guadalcanal.

Army soldiers push through the same sort of jungle undergrowth that
survivors had to negotiate.

The F4F Wildcat single seat fighter.

A two-man raft becomes a four-man raft in this simulated ditching exercise.

The crew of a Navy TBM scrambles out of its aircraft after ditching next to an aircraft carrier.

The confusion, sharp edges, rushing water, and countless ways that things got snagged on something created a maelstrom of challenges just to get free of one's plane.

The business end of an American air attack on a Japanese base.

The codenames for the names of Japanese freighters were based on the number of holds they had as evidenced by the number of masts. These appear to be Sugar Dogs, two-masted ships with two large holds.

A B-17 slams into the water during a controlled crash test.

A B-24 seen after a controlled ditching. Even on flat seas the forces of a ditching often tore apart an aircraft.

The white cliffs of Dover. A welcome sight for an aircraft limping home. To the left is the English Channel.

This B-29 ditched short of the runway and is seen in the water as men swim out to help the crew.

The belly of an albatross was an unexpected source of food for many downed pilots. The bird was large enough to be relatively easy to shoot with a handgun.

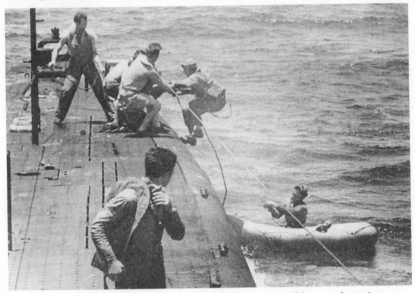

A downed Kingfish pilot, usually the rescuer, is rescued by a submarine.

In a small one-man raft, the submarine Finback comes alongside President George H.W. Bush.

The Martin PBM Mariner. PBMs were truly versatile, bombing Japanese ships and shore installations or used in air-sea rescue.

The Kingfisher floatplane could be either be ship based or land based. From a ship it was fired off a catapult and hoisted back aboard by crane.

The PBY Catalina. Originally designed to find and attack Japanese transports, the Cat became the workhorse of air-sea rescue.

The crew of a downed bomber makes its way towards a Catalina. Oftentimes one of the crew members had to stay in the water while the others beat off the sharks.

A airdropped rescue boat descends near a B-17 that has ditched.

A charcoal drawing of a crew that is safe in its life raft as their plane goes under.

Bombers carried their larger life rafts in compartments behind the engines.

Two-man life raft tethered together. Note the CO2 bottles in front.

A downed crewman (simulated) grabs a float and will be reeled in to a raft.

The survivors from a crashed bomber climb aboard the wings of this Kingfisher presumably saving them from sharks.

13

FOOTPRINTS ON THE BEACH

Experience of Ensign Lawty, USNR, _____, from July 17 to August 3, 1943 as told to Air Combat Intelligence Office, Halavo Seaplane Base.

****

The night of July 16-17 eight destroyers went up the slot to evacuate survivors of the "STRONG" and "HELENA" who had made their way to shore on Vella Layella. One P-plane section of TBFs was air cover from 2300 to 0100, and Lt. (jg) Champlin and I in two more TPFs were supposed to relieve them on station and protect the cans from 0100 to 0300.

We took off from Henderson Field at 0000, but as soon as I was airborne I discovered I had no radio contact with Champlin, so I returned to base and got another plane and proceeded up the slot alone. I arrived on station shortly after one and stayed there until 0300, making no contacts, not even a Black Cat. We were told to keep away from the cans so of course I didn't see them. I was in radio communication with Champlin, however, and at 0300 he reported he was returning to base, so I headed for home.

After flying awhile I saw Vangunu and a little later thought I saw the Russells, but it may have been a cloud shadow. You know how hard it is to spot landmarks on a dark night.

My radar was out—there weren't any fuses in it when I took off. About 0430 I thought I was south of Guadalcanal. I heard Champlin asking for landing instructions and I called the tower myself requesting searchlights so I could get my bearings, but couldn't raise the tower. Up to then my radio communications had been excellent.

I saw a coastline on my port beam and decided to take a reciprocal course but I soon ran into clouds. I climbed in order to get into the beam and soon picked it up, the beam indicating I was south of Guadalcanal. I took a 033° heading and after a short while figured I should be over Henderson. I was flying at 10,000 feet at the time.

I tried to get Henderson Tower again and this time I raised them but reception was poor. I asked for illumination and they said the searchlights were on. At 10,000 feet it was getting light about that time and besides there was a thick overcast below me and I couldn't see the lights.

The tower told me to stand by and continue on that heading. I realized then that I was lost. I continued on 033° heading for a while, dropping my bombs to save gas, and then took a reciprocal heading. It was quite light at that time. I was awfully low on gas, so I started letting down. The tower reported that I was bearing 000° from Henderson so I headed 180°.

Both my wing tanks were dry by then and my last tank was registering empty. I put my radioman in the second cockpit and sometime between 0630 and 0645 made a power water landing with flaps down and wheels up.

My gunner got out of the port escape hatch and got the raft out and inflated it. I got out of the cockpit, keeping my parachute, .45 automatic, a knife, first aid kit and my canteen. My canteen was empty—I drink a lot of water on those night flights—but I also salvaged a ditty bag of provisions containing two canteens and some chocolate bars.

While I was swimming around in the water my head got caught in the plane's radio antenna and the shroud lines of the chute entangled my feet, but I could see Stott, the radioman, was bleeding and was groggy so I managed to swim over and get him out of the second cockpit.

Waldheim, the gunner, in the meanwhile had the raft and oars all set. The tail of the plane, as it went down, caught the raft and put a small puncture in the inner tubing and a large tear in the outer cover, breaking the raft's life line and knocking off the kit of raft provisions.

The raft was partially deflated by the puncture and we no sooner got in than a swell capsized it. I was still tangled in my chute shrouds and in trying to get back in the raft I lost my ditty bag of provisions.

We tried to pump up the raft but had little success. It was unmaneuverable so we just floated. We expected a rescue plane at any time since Henderson knew our position. The only food at hand was two chocolate bars and we shared one of them.

About 0830 we saw two B-25s pass about two mile away. We thought they were searching for us and we were disappointed when they went right on. They returned several hours later but still didn't see us.

That afternoon we saw more B-25s and two or three single engine craft —possibly returning from a strike.

At noon of the second day (July 18th) a squall enabled us to fill our canteen and cup. We had a good drink and ate our second chocolate bar. We had seen some planes that morning and fired .45 tracers but it hadn't done any good. We couldn't see land anywhere. We started paddling south, judging direction as well as we could from the sun, but it was no dice, so we put out a sea anchor made out of the parachute. The wind was against us for sailing.

The morning of the third day (July 19th) we began to realize we might be at sea some time and we managed to pump up the raft. It seemed to seal itself when it was inflated and required very little pumping after that to keep it full of air. We rigged a sail when the wind was favorable or paddled until we were tired, heading south all the time.

On the fourth morning (July 20th) we sighted land for the first time. It was due south and we kept heading towards it although we didn't have any idea what island it was. We had no more water, but that night there was a squall and we were able to fill our canteen again, using our Mae Wests to catch the rain.

The following day (July 21st) we saw several more points of land rising from the water. They seemed to be mountain peaks on one big island but it could have been the westerly end of Santa Isabel and the easterly end of Choiseul—we couldn't tell.

We paddled hard all day long, making definite progress. Planes came near us every day we were on the water—at least one each morning and afternoon. At dark that evening of the fifth day we believed we could make land in 24 hours. Between sunset and moonrise we lashed our paddles and shoes to the raft and rested. When we wanted to start paddling again we found that one of the paddles and one of Waldheim's shoes had been lost.

On the sixth morning (July 22nd) a B-24 flew directly over us at low altitude. We waved at him and he banked and circled. He dropped smoke bombs and blinked "help coming." We replied by semaphore "OK" and asked him to drop provisions and water, but he apparently didn't get our message.

The B-24 hung around one and a half to two hours. We were very happy because rescue was so near, so we put out our sea anchor, went in swimming and lay on the raft sunbathing to ease the salt water sores on our legs and tails.

Some time after the B-24 had left, a PBY showed up about half a mile away. He circled into the wind at 250 feet altitude and we were sure he was getting ready to let down his wing tip floats and land. But then he turned south towards land again.

Stott fashioned a paddle from a can of repair gear and we headed towards the islands once more. We had drifted beyond the northern tip of Santa Isabel by then. That afternoon another PBY passed within two miles but didn't see us.

The morning of the seventh day (July 23rd) a third PBY came in night but passed by. By noon the wind was favorable to sailing south so we sailed until about an hour after sundown, setting said again at moonrise.

At sunrise, July 24th, we seemed to be about a half hour from land which we took to be the northeast coast of Choiseul. We could see cover, beaches and small coconut plantations on shore. However, we were farther out at sea then we realized since it wasn't until about 1000—three to four hours later—that we finally reached shore on a wide sandy beach not far from a plantation. We lost our improvised paddle when the surf carried our boat over the coral reef but once we were inside the lagoon we got into the water and swam, pushing our raft the half mile to shore.

On the beach we saw fresh bare footprints. We were pretty weak and feeble but we were taking no chances and we dragged our raft up the beach and hid it in the bush. We were all surprised at how feeble we were—it was almost impossible to walk.

We made our way to the edge of the plantation finally and tried to open coconuts but we were too weak and couldn't do it. We returned to the raft and hid all our flight gear, but there was no food there so we decided to go back to the plantation and take a chance of running into Japs.

As we came close to the plantation we sighted two natives and called to them, but they ran to the beach and put out from shore in a canoe. While I scouted the plantation buildings, Stott and Waldheim tried to reassure the natives we meant no harm and they finally were able to persuade them we were white and friendly, so they came ashore.

One of them was the plantation owner—a native named Venga who spoke pidgin fairly well. They fed us coconut milk, breadfruit, and bananas and gave us water to drink. They sent a third native as a messenger to the coastwatchers while they put us in a canoe and paddled a mile up the coast, then inland up a river to a native village which we reached about 1300.

There they fed us some more and we bathed in a mountain stream. After about an hour, two of the coastwatcher's armed native police arrived. One of them—Peter—spoke fair pidgin but the other—Gordon Pambulu— spoke good English. Pambulu questioned us and then said "we are your friends, we have the U. S. Government issue," and produced a can of Spam. It was undeniable proof.

We ate some more, smoked cigarettes they had brought, and rested. After a while we proceeded to the coastwatcher's headquarters. In our condition it was about a two hour trip—our feet were sore from sunburn and Waldheim and I were barefoot. We arrived about 1700.

Pambulu had studied medicine for four years in Fiji and he dressed our sores and bathed our feet in Epson salts. No praise is too great for that man —he had a good professional manner and he was extremely careful and patient and considerate in his care of us.

The coastwatcher welcomed us and had a cooked dinner prepared for us. We told him how glad we were to be picked up. That night after listening to news on the radio we went to bed. The beds were sort of tables made with bamboo slats covered with a tarp and a good mattress.

Well, I dreamed and I rolled and pitched all night long. I woke up every hour clinging to the sides of my bed but I never had such wonderful dreams before in my life—I was at home, with friends, going to cocktail parties, a lot of pretty girls around. During the night I made a complete turn so that in the morning my head was where my feet had been.

Waldheim must have had a pretty good night too, because I could hear him laughing out loud every so often. Stott must have been having trouble, though, because I heard him screaming about "box cars" (B-24s).

We stayed there from July 23rd until Dumbo picked us up ten days later.

14

DYNAMITE A BRIDGE ON THE WAY OUT

On the morning of 15 December 1944 the planes of Task Force Thirty-eight were on the job to continue the work started the day before. The Japanese Air Force was being kept on the ground by a constant patrol of all the airfields on Luzon, and their planes were being sought for in their deviously camouflaged hideouts and destroyed. On the first flight of the day from the U.S.S. *Hancock*, Lt. Hickey, a VF-7 pilot, who gives the following account of his exploits:

Flying over the assigned area, we found no airborne opposition, so we proceeded to check over the fields for grounded aircraft. As I was making my second strafing run on the dispersal area of Porac airfield my plane was hit by AA. The oil and hydraulic pressure dropped to zero and the battery and generator failed. This, coupled with the improper responding of the controls and the smoke starting to fill the cockpit, made an immediate landing unavoidable. The only injuries to myself were several small shrapnel wounds in my right leg just below the knee. Managing to get about eight miles west of Porac, I made a wheels up landing on a trail on a ridge. As soon as I landed I flipped the detonator switch on the IFF, but it failed to function due to the power failure. As I climbed out of the plane I notice a group of men coming towards me so I started legging it out for the bushes and waved to my circling wingman as I went. Looking back, I saw some women with the men and observed that no one was in uniform so I figured they were civilians and came back. They knew I was an American and marched me off to a nearby hill where I was presented with three raw eggs —not quite up to the meals I was used to, but I learned to eat them. On the hill we held a discussion in broken English, with me wanting to go back and burn the plane and them wanting to take out the usable parts, assuring me all the time that it was safe from the Japanese. It was finally agreed that I would stay on the hill while they went back and removed the guns and ammunition and burned the plane. At 1300, while they were busy removing the gear and running back and forth to get more detailed instructions, a flight of F6Fs from the ship appeared on the scene. I tried to signal from the hill, but to no avail, so the plane was destroyed by a direct hit with an incendiary bomb. As the pilots could see figures leaving the plane as they approached, they decided they were Japs so they strafed the gulleys. This sad event resulted in one civilian being killed and three others injured. With the equipment in my backpack I gave the wounded men first aid treatment and did some fast talking to explain the actions of my shipmates. Having treated my own shrapnel wounds, also, I made quite an impression on the fellow who was to be my guide and I was later asked to help deliver a baby, but luckily escaped that task. In every town I was requested to treat the children who had large tropical ulcers. I should have been a doctor as it paid dividends in good will.

Before starting out for the guerrilla headquarters, I opened my concentrated food, but it didn't last long. The fellow that was to be my guide said it would take two days to get across to the Eastern side of the island, but this turned out to be a gross understatement. We walked all that night even though it rained and the ridges between the rice paddies were slippery. Early on the morning of the sixteenth we reached a small village where, with the "open sesame" and "Americano," we were taken into a house, fed rice and raw eggs and given a mat to sleep on. This night traveling and day time sleeping continued for six days. During this time I collected a lot of intelligence information about the Japanese which I hoped to be able to get out in time to be of value. Most of the traveling was done on foot, but native draft animals called "caribou" and canoes were occasionally used. One night I had a four hour canoe trip through a Niepa swamp. It was more of a mud sled ride than a canoe ride, as there was insufficient water in the swamp to float the canoe and it was pushed by boys. I tried to help them but only succeeded in almost tipping the boat over so I tried to sleep and to kill the millions of insects between naps. During this time I met one American woman who had married a Filipino lawyer. It was a welcome sight to see a white face again and to talk to someone without having to use my hands. The shrapnel wounds had caused my leg to become swollen, but four sulfa pills a day soon relieved it and walking was made easier.

The twenty-second of December we reached a fishing town where we slept all day while being stared at by twenty old women and fifty children. That night a Chinese boy got me a large bottle of Japanese adabrine and some sulfa powder. The latter had been sent by the Red Cross to those imprisoned on Luzon. He had gotten the material through a little shrewd trading with the Japs. The following day I arrived at the guerrilla headquarters. Here I had a much-needed rest, some good rice, well-educated people to talk to, and an escape from crying babies. Christmas day we had pig for dinner and I received a pair of Japanese wool socks—one of the most appreciated Christmas presents that I have ever gotten.

On the morning of 27 December I left the headquarters and traveled most of the day hidden in the bottom of a native canoe. In the evening my guides and I picked up an armed squadron of about seventy-five men near San Simon and kept going on foot. During the night we passed through a small village which we could not go around and here we encountered an eight-man Jap patrol enforcing the curfew. The Japanese were ambushed and killed. Every type of gun, from the old long barrel single shot to a Thompson sub-machine gun, was used. As soon as the patrol had fallen everyone rushed up and grabbed what arms and other valuables they could and started running and kept it up for three hours. Every time I would start to drag behind someone would shout "Jap" and I would quicken my step. I guess they were about as scared as I was. I really appreciated my new socks that night.

The twenty-eighth found me at a small fishing village on Manila Bay. After getting some food and rest I spent a couple of hours talking to a couple of the fishermen, persuading them into sailing me down to Mindoro. They weren't too eager about the trip but agreed to try it. The following morning two fishermen and I, with some rice, water, and three partially cooked chickens, set sail. We didn't get very far and after five hours we neared Corregidor Island and the submariner met buoys or mines—we weren't sure which they were. In either case it put an end to the trip and we turned back, reaching shore at 0300 the next day. I slept on most of the return trip.

There are two underground forces on Luzon, one in the plains called Kukbalahup or People's Anti-Japanese Army, the other in the mountains being the USFFE led by Major Anderson. These two forces were carrying on a civil war of their own when they weren't fighting the Japs. Each side was convinced that the other force was a bunch of thieves and murderers. I found out for myself how unfriendly the relations were when I and my two guides reached Meycauayan on the last day of the year. Here we found a battle taking place. I didn't really enjoy hiding behind the ridges and brush and seeing the bullets splash in the rice paddies behind me. That night we moved around the area of the fighting and through civilian guides were turned over to the USFFE. Even though the two groups carried on this feud they didn't hesitate to turn me over from one outfit to another when they thought it would better my chances of escape.

On New Year's day I received another welcome present—a toothbrush. The next two nights were spent walking and on the third we traveled in the daylight, having reached the hills where there were no Japs and few civilians.

On the fourth we arrived at Victory Hill, the headquarters for the USFFE. The Commanding Officer and his staff sent a radio message to Leyte for me to be forwarded to VF-7 and to my family. Here I met a Lt. Fulkerson who was a P-38 pilot, two U.S. demolition officers, and a man who had escaped from a concentration camp after his capture on Bataan. The next day a B-25 dropped some concentrated food and demolition supplies. Until the eighth my newly-acquired friends and I did nothing but eat, rest, and attend one short class in "The Art of Demolition."

The morning of the eighth, Lt. Fulkerson; Lt. Campbell, who was the demolition expert; and I set out on a mission to blow up the railroad bridge at Diliman, as the Japs had repaired the bridge at Plaridel which had been destroyed a few days previously. Between the three of us we carried about 90 lbs. of TNT caps and fuses plus two Thompson sub-machine guns, a carbine and three 45s. We were really all set to fight the war.

The Jap patrol had to check two bridges which were a mile apart so this gave us about 30 minutes to set the charges, but it only took us 20 minutes to do the job and at 2220 we set off a terrific explosion. We later heard, though the grapevine, that the Japs had a little trouble moving troops from Manila to Cabanatuan the next day when General MacArthur made his landings. We returned to Victory Hill and lived the life of ease again for several days.

On the twelfth we received word over the radio at HQ that there were L-5s on the strip at Lingayen. Lt. Fulkerson and I toyed with the idea of constructing a small strip down near the burned and abandoned town of Akle. By the fourteenth we had gotten tired of sitting around so we went down to the valley and marked out a strip. We decided on an open field and a section of a banana plantation. The next five days were spent in working on our strip, 20 x 240 yards. Thanks to the natives, their caribou and the rains, we had a serviceable job. The latter was done with an old plow, a harrow, and home-made roller, and the nightly rains packed it for us.

On the eighteenth, three pilots, including Col. Atkinson, and two aircrewmen stopped on their way up to the USFFE H.Q. Our pleas for planes during the past days had been unanswered but on the morning of the 20th four P-38s flying cover and two L-5s appeared over the area and the two small planes made a beautiful landing. Our hopes hit a new high. Col. Atkinson was on Victory Hill so we convinced the pilots that they could fly us out and be back by the time the runner got up to H.Q. and back. This was a little exaggeration but we wanted to get out. Nine Americans were taken out via this route in two days. The Army interrogated me and treated me like a long-lost son and with air priorities I went to Mindoro, Palau, and Ulithi where I joined VF-7 again just forty-one days after I left.

15

THE ENGLISH CHANNEL

Ditching was not reserved to the Pacific Theater. The heaviest traffic was between England and Germany over the English Channel. At its narrowest point, rescue could come in minutes. Elsewhere, the distances were much greater. But no matter where, the weather and the fog were two serious problems; and despite the tight confines, crews could drift for days. Here are stories representative of the trials and tribulations of the aircrews that went down in the English Channel.

****

PART 1: D-DAY

The ditching of a C-47A aircraft, serial number 42-92845, of the 314th Troop Carrier Group, occurred at 0010 hours, 6 June 1944, at approximately 50° N, 03° W, about 60 miles SE of Start Point. The personnel involved in the ditching consisted of 18 paratroopers and the aircraft crew of six, including a radar observer.

****

Events Preceding Ditching

The aircraft, participating in the invasion operation on D-Day, was hit by flak on reaching mainland coast after passing between two of the Channel

Islands. Flak bursts damaged the left engine, leaving only the right engine serviceable. The right engine was burning out rapidly because of the excess power required to maintain flight.

The pilot realized he would have to ditch because of the flak damage. He issued orders, therefore, to prepare for ditching. All loose equipment, including parachutes, was jettisoned. The pilot desired to ditch off the German-held islands because he had been fired upon by friendly surface vessels in the Sicilian operation, but the co-pilot favored locating and ditching alongside a naval craft. It was decided to land near a surface vessel, and the radar operator successfully guided them to a British destroyer.

VHF distress calls were made to the Air/Sea Rescue Fixer Service and to other planes in the group, but were probably not received because of low altitude. An MF call was also sent, but no reply was received from the MF/DF Station, again probably because of low altitude. IFF was turned to the distress position two minutes before contact.

The final approach was made during darkness, using landing lights, from 100 feet at 100 mph, using full flaps until just before contact, when the flaps were raised completely. Setdown was made between 85 and 90 mph without power, directly into the swell. The aircraft was landed into the wind with the tail well down and level laterally. Final impact was moderate, though the radar antenna and the cowling on the right engine broke off during the landing. The aircraft came to rest in a tail-high attitude at an angle of about 45 degrees. There was approximately one foot of water in the cockpit and six inches of water in the cabin when the last man left the airplane. The Dakota floated for 20 minutes and sank nose first.

All personnel left via the cargo door except the co-pilot , who remained in the cockpit, signaling to the destroyer with a flashlight. He eventually climbed out of the upper escape hatch, caught a rope thrown from the destroyer, and walked off the wing into the boat without getting wet.

The other members inflated their life vests before leaving the aircraft. They used their two type A-3 rafts and one British type J dinghy.

The pilot praised the excellent discipline displayed by the paratroopers. No one moved from his seat until told to do so by the jumpmaster, when they got up six at a time and jumped from the rear door into the water so as to avoid any damage to the life rafts.

The personnel were only in their life rafts from 10 to 15 minutes before they were immediately picked up by the British destroyer. They suffered very slightly from the immersion, and no steps were taken to overcome this problem until aboard the destroyer.

Paratrooper personnel assumed ditching stations in their normal position—that is, in the bucket seats with safety belts fastened. This proved to be very satisfactory, as no one was injured during or after the ditching.

Radar-equipped aircraft have a distinct advantage during this type of operation when used intelligently. Locating the destroyer was probably the major contributing factor to the complete success of this incident.

PART 2: DITCHING A B-17

The ditching of a B-17G aircraft, serial number 42-31208, of the 447th Bombardment Group occurred at 1405 hours, 9 March 1944, at approximately 52°N, 04°E, 10 miles off the coast of Holland.

The aircraft was returning from an operational mission, flying at 16,000 feet, when the No. 2 engine ran out of gas, though the gauge still registered 60 gallons. Power settings were increased to 2300 rpm and 38 inches manifold pressure in order to stay with the formation. Approximately ten minutes later the No. 3 engine ran out of gas, the gauge still registering 40 gallons. After the loss of No. 3, all excess equipment, including guns and ammunition, was jettisoned. The aircraft gradually began to lag behind the formation, and the group leader was called and informed of the impending emergency. Altitude could not be maintained, and a gradual descent became necessary. Ten minutes later scattered flak came through under cast, but no damage resulted. No. 1 engine ran out of gas about five minutes later, the gauge reading about 50 gallons. Pilot then informed the crew he would have to ditch. The navigator gave the radio operator a position, and then followed the bombardier and enlisted personnel to the radio room to assume their ditching positions. Altitude was then about 10,000 feet. The IFF toggle switch was turned to emergency position, and an SOS was sent out on the M/F frequency by the radio operator. The radio message was delayed about 10 seconds because another aircraft was sending an SOS, but when the MF/DF section was contacted, a fix was obtained. Pilot called "MAYDAY" on D-channel, and gave a long count so a fix could be obtained.

VHF calls were repeated every few minutes until ditching. A steep glide was started from 10,000 feet, and No. 4 engine continued to operate until the setdown was accomplished.

Just before ditching, the pilot and co-pilot opened their windows about six inches. The top turret guns were pointed forward, and just before taking his ditching position, the radio operator clamped down on the radio key, though he continued to stand by on interphone. Emergency equipment the crew planned to take into the raft was placed against the rear of the radio compartment. The radio operator took his ditching position of the left side under the radio table, lying on his back with his feet against the forward bulkhead, and the navigator assumed a similar position to the right of the radio operator. The bombardier sat with his back to the forward door in the radio room, his head braced against the door. The tail gunner sat with his back to the bombardier's legs, and the engineer sat against the tail gunner's legs. The left waist gunner sat to the right of the bombardier with his back to the forward wall, his head against the wall. The right waist gunner sat against the legs of the left waist gunner, and the ball turret gunner sat against the right waist gunner's legs. All crew members, with the exception of the navigator and radio operator, doubled up their legs and clasped their hands behind their heads to prevent any possible injury from the shock of alighting. At the time of ditching there was a 7- to 10-knot wind from 20 degrees, and visibility was about a mile. There was an overcast, and the weather seemed to be closing in rapidly. Waves were about six feet high, and the swell was not perceptible until coming close to the water.

The aircraft was flattened out about five feet above the water, and landed in a slightly tail-down attitude, using one-third flaps. There was an initial shock as the tail dragged through the water, followed by a severe shock when the nose made contact. Water was forced up through the camera well into the radio room, and the ball turret tore loose and crashed through the radio room door, but did not injure anyone. However, the navigator injured his jaw on the leg of the radio table.

The crew climbed out of the radio room through the escape hatch, and released the life rafts externally. The pilot and co-pilot escaped through their respective windows, using the top turret guns to get out and onto the wings. Five men boarded each dinghy, with the bombardier, navigator, right waist gunner, and engineer in one and the remaining crew members in the other. Both dinghies were shoved off at the same time, and the crew paddled them to the rear of the aircraft, where they tied the rafts together. Using the oars of the dinghies, the crews paddled about 100 feet from the port side, and waited there until it went down so they could retrieve the emergency radio, which was floating underneath the tail. At 1641, 36 minutes after hitting the water, the aircraft submerged, and the radio was picked up shortly thereafter.

The crew tried to launch the dinghy kite, but were unsuccessful because of insufficient wind. The crew then inflated one of the rubber balloons to a diameter of approximately 30 inches, but found it would not hold up the antenna. The other balloon was then inflated to a diameter of about 42 inches, and the two of them were tied together and the aerial let out. SOS was transmitted, using the Auto I position on the dinghy radio. About 20 minutes later a Hudson bomber appeared, and the crew fired signal flares. The bomber approached and dropped an airborne lifeboat, which landed about 80 feet from the dinghies, and the crew paddled to the lifeboat and transferred from the dinghy. The balloons and aerial were lost during the transfer. All excess equipment was placed in the rubber dinghies, which were tied behind the lifeboat. After circling for half an hour, the bomber flashed a heading for steering to the English coast, and then left in that direction. Soon after boarding the lifeboat, the crew found two kapok flotation suits, and the navigator, who was injured, and the right waist gunner, who was wet and cold, were dressed in these. The next morning a third kapok suit was found and worn by the pilot, but the remaining four suits, which were supposed to be part of the equipment, were never found. After the Hudson left, the weather started closing in, and with darkness approaching, the crew members made themselves as comfortable as possible underneath the bow and stern buoyancy chambers. However, the stern chamber had not inflated when the boat hit the water. Because of darkness and the fact that the bomber had located their position, the crew concentrated on keeping warmer, feeling sure that the rescue boats would come out before the night expired.

In the early hours of morning, when no signs of rescue were apparent, the mast was raised and dinghy radio attached thereto. The ship antenna was not attached because its existence was not known. The sails were then hoisted, the compass was fixed in position, and an attempt was made to sail in the proper direction. By use of the sail and rudder, headings of 180 degrees to 250 degrees were the closest that could be maintained to the 280 degrees given by the bomber. An unsuccessful attempt was then made to start the gasoline engines. At first it was found impossible to turn the flywheel in the proper direction because the cylinders were filled with water. The water was pumped out and plugs cleaned and replayed, but another unsuccessful attempt to start the engines resulted. The lifeboat's emergency radio was brought out, and an attempt was made to launch the lifeboat kite with the rocket pistol. This failed, and the kite landed in the water about 50 feet from the boat. The kite was then taken into the back of the boat, and another unsuccessful attempt was made to fly the kite by hand. Another attempt to start the engines failed. Shortly after noon, the second kite was unfolded and attempts were made to fly it, and eventually the kite floated into the air. The lifeboat's radio antenna was then attached and let out to its complete length. After an unsuccessful attempt was made to tune up the lifeboat radio, the dinghy radio was attached to the aerial. The dinghy radio was tuned up successfully and was cranked for approximately one hour, at which time two air-sea rescue boats were seen heading toward the boat from the horizon.

The rescue boats drew up alongside the airborne lifeboat, and the crew was transferred. Soon after being taken aboard, the rescue boat radio operator received a message from the land station saying that emergency signals had been received and a new fix obtained. Although the rescue boats found the crew while sailing a search pattern, the new fix obtained from the dinghy radio would have resulted in their locating the crew.

Weather Conditions

1. Sea with long rolling swell, waves reputed to be 40 feet high, wind approximately 12 m.p.h., visibility good.
2. The pilot and second pilot stayed in their flying positions and remaining crew were placed—7 in the radio compartment, and the other members of the crew braced against the aft radio room bulkhead opposite the under ball turret. An S.O.S. Procedure was attempted, but the wireless

was seen to be out of order. An approach was made across a heavy swell at 100 m.p.h. with flaps fully lowered. On impact the aircraft was broken into four pieces as follows.

3. Both wings came adrift and the fuselage broke in half at the center of the bomb cell. The deceleration must have been fairly large, as the radio room bomb bay bulkhead was thrust forward three to four feet by the weight of aircrew which were braced against it. The under ball turret was forced upwards into the fuselage and narrowly missed causing severe injury to the Observer, who was braced near this turret.

4. The dinghies were not released, but floated out of the wreckage, together with the 7 members of the aircrew who had been stationed in the center part of the fuselage. The pilot and second pilot effected their exits through the port and starboard flying cabin windows. All 10 members of the aircrew managed to get away from the wreckage, and both dinghies were found and attempts made to inflate them. As these dinghies had not been stowed in their official stowage positions but wrapped in string and stowed—1 in the Radio Cabin and the other in the aft part of the fuselage—extreme difficulty was experienced in the attempt to effect inflation. The time taken by the aircrew to inflate the first dinghy was 30 minutes. In the meantime, three members of the aircrew were drowned, although wearing American "Mae Wests".

5. During this first 30 minutes, one member of the aircrew grabbed hold of a floating object to give himself buoyancy. It was found to be the dinghy radio and kite launching apparatus. The 7 surviving members of the crew managed to get aboard the first dinghy, and after an interval of 5 minutes, the second dinghy was inflated. Although no previous practice had been experienced by any members of the aircrew with the dinghy wireless, the kite was suitably launched by hand and the aerial attached, and an S.O.S. was automatically transmitted. A fix was made on the S.O.S. transmitted and after a period of 6 hours, Air/Sea Rescue aircraft sighted the distressed aircrew and a Lindholme Rescue gear was dropped.

6. The aircrew managed to paddle to the Lindholme Dinghy and make themselves more comfortable, availing themselves of comforts and pyrotechnics from the containers attached to the dinghy. After a further

period of 2 hours, the aircrew were rescued by a Minesweeper which had been diverted for this purpose.

Part 3: They'll Take Luck Any Day

The preceding is yet another outstanding example of amazing luck in spite of lack of correct training. The aircraft was returning from a bombing raid on 4 March 1943. At 22,000 feet, the aircraft was engaged by enemy aircraft. In the ensuing action, three engines and the radio were put out of action. The aircraft proceeded on its course, losing height steadily— engagement ensuing down to 5,000 feet. This loss of 17,000 feet took approximately half an hour. At 5,000 feet, the pilot decided that a ditching was imminent and certain loose equipment was jettisoned, including port and starboard waist guns and remaining ammunition. An attempt was made to jettison equipment from the nose of the machine but the aircrew was unable to open the hatch.

Part 4: Roughman Red

On the 9th of April, 1944, I was flying in Roughman Red Flight #2 position. When we made landfall (L/F), my wing tanks ran dry, so I dropped them. I noticed a smell of gas in the oxygen system, but gave it no thought. Soon afterwards, Skybird called to withdraw from the bombers. I removed my oxygen mask and smelled the cockpit. It smelled of gas, and I realized the possibility of a fuel leak. I still had plenty of gas, so I was not worried. I switched my oxygen to the "Off" position which eliminated the smell of gas.

Captain Byers, my flight leader, and I spotted an a/f, and I hoped we would attack it, which we did. No. 3 and No. 4 of the flight gave us top cover while we went down. I was slightly higher and about 1/2 mile's line abreast of Capt. Byers when an FW 190 went between us in the opposite direction. Capt. Byers told me that it was an FW and I turned upon it as it made a 180 degree turn to go after Capt. Byers. When the e/a saw me he turned into me and we exchanged fire head-on, no hits. I pushed everything forward and went into a sharp climbing turn to make another pass at the e/a. I out-turned him but could not get enough deflection on him. We exchanged fire again, and I observed no hits. The e/a broke off the attack and headed West. I decided to chase him and was gaining on him until I hit detonation. I was running an automatic lean. Before I broke off my pursuit, I was about one mile behind him so I gave him about two rings' vertical deflection and fired a burst. I noticed him turning to the left and flying closer to the ground. I turned around and took a heading of 240 degrees and flew on the deck until I made L/F out and climbed up to 8,000 ft. Capt. Byers tried to locate me during the engagement but I had gone inland too far for him to do so. I ran out of oxygen at that time and the odor of gas fumes was terrific. I had about 140 gallons of gas left and figured that I might make it. I throttled back to 30" of mercury and 1500 RPM. As my gas was going down fast, I took a heading of 248 degrees and flew along the Frisian Islands as was planned. It was hazy and I could not tell exactly where I was and how much further I had to fly before leaving the islands. As I noticed my gas going down further, I pulled back to 1400 RPM and knew then that I would not be able to make it home. I do not remember what time that was. I thought of expending all my ammunition and did so. Some 10 or 15 minutes later, I was indicating 40 gallons of gas and called anyone in Roughman Squadron if they could find me so that I could have an escort until I bailed out. Lt. Maguire's flight turned back and found me. I called for Mayday but could not be heard. While Lt. Stanley, Lt. Crampton and Lt. Furness flew alongside of me, Lt. Maguire gained altitude and tried to call for Mayday. They received him and told us to fly a course of 260 degrees. I tried again to call Tackline control. They would receive me but could not get a fix on me at the time. Lt. Maguire called again a few seconds later and they did get a fix and told me to fly a course of 255 degrees.

My gas was down to 30 gallons. I tried to remain calm while Lt. Maguire continued to call a Mayday for me. We had left the islands about five minutes before this. My gas gauge remained at 30 gallons for about 10 minutes when the engine quit. I switched to my auxiliary tank to see if I could get any gas out of it, but it was dry. I got a surge of power and the engine quit again. I switched to main again, got another surge of power and the engine quit again. I switched back to auxiliary—no gas. Switched back to main—no gas. I gave Tackline a last call and told them I was bailing out. I also said so long to the fellows who were escorting me. I was at 5,000 ft. and had plenty of time, so I unloosened all connections to my body and tried to roll the ship over on its back which I think I should not have done. The ship

went into a split "S", shuddered and started to spin. At that time, I let everything go and climbed out the right side. As I was getting out, I saw myself
sliding along the fuselage towards the tail assembly. I grabbed the right side
of the canopy with my right hand and pressed myself against the fuselage
with my left hand, and as I climbed out, my feet were slammed against the
fuselage. I pressed my feet against the fuselage and pushed away from the a/
c going down backwards. I believe my left little finger hit the horizontal stabilizer. I received no jolt when I pulled my rip cord. I seated myself well in
the chute and undid the leg harness. As I got near the water, I undid my
chest strap. I was descending slowly and I entered the water in a sitting position, releasing myself from the chute and inflating my Mae West at the same
time.

I did not go under water at all. I had no trouble getting into my dinghy,
thanks to my dinghy drill some several months ago. The water was rather
cold and even after I got into my dinghy and bailed all the water out, I shivered all the while. Lts Maguire, Crampton, Stanley and Furness must have
stayed with me for about 2 hours. Their buzzing and circling around me was
a great morale factor. They were like God watching over head. Before they
had to leave, another ship arrived over me and took over. The weather was
closing in faster and I could see this plane going in and out of the fog. It led
me to believe he lost sight of me. I tried using my flares. As the roar of the
engine got louder, I pulled the pin in the first flare, it did not work. I tried
that 3 times; all three flares failed to work. I did not know whether he lost
sight of me, but things began to look black. The weather was getting bad
and I was preparing myself for an all night stand. I emptied my escape kit
and put the different things in different pockets so that I would know where
to find what I wanted at night. I chewed a piece of gum which helped. I tried
a Malted Milk tablet but it seemed to make me more thirsty. However, food
and water did not concern me much at the time. About 4 hours after I was
in the dinghy, 2 bombers passed overhead. I waved the flag I had but they
did not see me. At each sound of a plane, I would look around to see where
it was, but could not find it. This discouraged me to no end. It got so that I
was too afraid to look for any more planes for fear they would be going in
another direction and discourage me some more. All this while I was trying
to make myself comfortable but could not do so. The water began to get

choppy and the weather worse. 3 more P-47s came out of the West, did a 180 degree turn around me and headed back West again. Whether or not they saw me I do not know. They gave me no indication of it. Things began to look blacker yet. Sometime later, I heard another a/c approaching, so I turned around to see if I could see it. He was circling nearby and as I looked West, I saw the silhouette of a gray launch approaching me head on from out of the mist. It was the prettiest sight any one could see. From there on it was smooth sailing, although it took me about 2 hours to thaw out and the injury to my left ankle became prominent.

My most profound appreciation and gratefulness to Lt. Maguire for his smart head work and determination, and also to Lts Stanley, Crampton, Furness and Lorance, and also to Lt. C.W.S. Sheppard and his crew of HMS *Midge* and all concerned in bringing about my rescue.

Herewith is a suggestion given to me by Lt. C.W.S. Sheppard of A.S.R. which I would like to pass on to those concerned.

In choppy water and poor weather, such as I experienced, a balloon, four or five feet in diameter, inflated with a lighter-than-air gas, and extended by a rope twenty to thirty feet long, would make a good marker in sighting the location of the dinghy.

Lt. Terzian

1st Lt., Air Corps

Perspective

Lt. Terzian called when just North of Emden. He said he had only 4 strikes, altitude 8,000 feet. He also asked if any Roughman ships had him in sight and give his approximate position. I turned around with 3 ships in my flight and sighted Lt. Terzian's ship North and East of us. Also sighted LF-I with Lt. Furness coming in from the East. We escorted Lt Terzian to North and West of Tessel Island and then changed over to B Channel with him. He stated that he had 30 gallons of fuel indicated. Lt. Terzian then gave two Maydays but was down to 6,500 feet and could not be reached. Three ships stayed with Lt. Terzian and I climbed to 8,000 feet and gave a successful Mayday. I was given a course of 260 degrees. Lt. Terzian carried on then for 3/4 minutes. He then called and said he thought he would have to bail out. I gave another Mayday and was given a course of 255 degrees. We followed this for another 3/4 minutes when Lt. Terzian's engine quit. He bailed out at 4,000 feet at about 1245 hours. I proceeded to give fixes, 1 about every 5 minutes after Lt. Terzian bailed out. Tackline told me to call Seagull 27 and vector him 330 degrees for 7 miles. Seagull acknowledged my message and said he was on his way. After 10 minutes I called Seagull 27 again and asked him if he had us sighted. He said that he could not see us but could hear us circling the dinghy. After another 4/5 minutes lapsed, Tackline said that two more spotters were on their way. He then asked me to give him a very long fix. Tackline then told me to call Seagull 27 again and to tell him to proceed to "H" as in How 111. 10 minutes later the spotters arrived and sighted Lt Terzian in the dinghy. We circled them for 5 more minutes and then headed out for home. After flying for 3 minutes, we sighted Seagull 27 but before we could head them for Lt. Terzian, we lost them in the haze. Visibility was only ¼ miles and when last seen, Seagull 27 was heading for the dinghy.

My flight consisted of Lt. Crampton, Lt. Stanley and Lt. Furness.

Lt. Maguire

1st Lt. Air Corps.

16

Surrounded in Hostile Waters

The following third-person report was filed on behalf of the crewmen involved.

****

On 7 June 1945, First Lieutenant D. B. Finch and Second Lieutenant J. G. Woliung, both of the 41st Fighter Squadron, 35thFighter Group, were in two of 10 P-51s scheduled to take off from Biak on a ferry mission to Clark Field, Luzon. Five of the planes were on Mainer Strip and Lts. Finch and Woliung were with three others on Berate Strip. They did not have fittings for the wing tanks on their two ships, so they took off at 1415/I. They circled Biak for thirty minutes waiting for the other flight of five ships, which was led by First Lieutenant Foster, 39th Fighter Squadron, 38thFighter Group. After a total of 45 minutes of circling, they proceeded through weather (scattered thunderheads) on a zigzag course. Lt. Foster's flight had full wing tanks. Lts. Finch and Woliung were pulling approximately 2000 RPM and 32 inches, and Lts. Finch's and Woliung's engines kept loading up abnormally, which necessitated their having to clear them regularly. After calling Lt. Foster and telling him to clear his engine, Lt. Finch's radio burned out. He did not have radio contact thereafter. The other flight did not seem to be clearing its engines and it was necessary for Lts. Finch and Woliung to do so. In order to do this and still remain with the other flight,

Lts. Finch and Woliung had to circle when clearing their engines. This procedure had used a large amount of gas when Lt. Finch decided to proceed ahead of Lt. Foster's flight. The two pilots "lined" themselves up with Lt. Foster's flight.

At about the time of their ETA, they encountered a front. They went down and looked under the front, but seeing that it looked clear over the top at 18,000 feet, they climbed over the front. Lt. Finch turned on his radio set try to pick up the base but to no avail. He tried at this time to turn on his emergency IFF, but was unable to do so, because the safety seal was wired down with three strands of copper wire and he was unable to break it. As a result, Lt. Finch received a finger injury trying to break it.

Lts. Finch and Woliung came down on the other side of the front, and now observed an island, and proceeded toward it to orientate themselves. Not having radio contact with one another, Lts. Finch and Woliung were forced to communicate by hand signals. Lt. Finch suspected the strange island to be Sangihe Island. Lt. Finch signaled Lt. Woliung that they were turning around, but Lt. Woliung pointed to his fuselage gas gauge and held up ten fingers and then five, indicating that he only 15 gallons of gas left. At the time, Lt. Finch had 20 gallons of gas but decided that it was not enough to return to Morotai, since it would be necessary to climb back over the front. Lt. Finch, thinking it wiser to stick together, signaled Lt. Woliung that they were going to ditch. They decided to ditch near the island in order to salvage as many necessities as they could from the planes. They found a reef near the island that seemed suitable.

In the meantime, unknown to Lt. Finch, Ft. Woliung, after learning that Lt. Finch's radio was out, tried to contact Applaud tower at Morotai, and all aircraft in its vicinity. Finallyhe succeeded in contacting a radio operator, giving the description of the island and their ditching position on the island. The radio operator acknowledged and said that he would transmit Lt. Woliung's message to Morotai.

At approximately 1830/I, Lts. Finch and Woliung ditched their planes off a reef in about five feet of water, and pulled their boats and jungle kits ashore. They planned to shove off and get away from the island, but the natives seemed very friendly and offered them food. Since they were on a remote and desolate section of the island, Lts. Finch and Woliung decide to chance spending the night on the beach at the water's edge with intentions of shoving off before daylight.

It had started to rain about 2000, so the two pilots took shelter in a boat house about 20 feet from shore. They had blown up their boats and were resting on them with one of their parachutes opened and spread over the top of them to dry their clothes. There were four natives sitting around them who appeared uninterested, so the confidence of the two pilots was built up. At approximately 2100, the natives prepared to leave. One of them lagged behind and the two pilots thought he said the word "hide". Lts. Finch and Woliung commented on it, for it appeared that it was the first English word they had heard any of the natives say. Approximately two minutes later they heard a commotion and looked up and saw approximately 10 figures approaching the front of the boat house. They started yelling and running toward the two pilots. Lts. Finch and Woliung sat up and immediately leveled their pistols, yelling, "Stop!" The figures stopped and retreated a few feet. Just then a flash of lightning revealed the ten figures kneeling a few feet from the shed with short rifles, similar to the Carbine. The "figures" then went back into the jungle and Lts. Finch and Woliung took their boats and other equipment to the water's edge. They had only been there a few minutes when the two "figures" (by now identified as, evidently, Japs) fired into the shed where they (Lts. Finch and Woliung) had been a moment before. The pilots grabbed their boats and rushed out into the water. The Japs opened fire in the direction of the two pilots with a machine gun. In the excitement, Lts. Finch and Woliung were unable to take any supplies with them excepting their two boats, a box of K-rations in the possession of Lt. Woliung, and one .45 pistol in the possession of Lt. Finch. Hoping that the Japs would not follow them if they knew that they were armed, Lt. Finch fired toward shore. The Japs did not follow, and the two pilots decided to put as much water, as possible, between them and land before morning. They tied their boats together and, since they had also lost their paddles, rowed with their hands all night. During the night the Japs and the natives built large bonfires for many miles along the coast on Sangihe Island.

At dawn, approximately 0630/I, the morning of 8 June, the two pilots were approximately eight miles away from their point of departure and about one mile east of Manipal Island (in the Sangihe group). They drifted and rowed periodically toward the open sea. At approximately 0900/I, they observed four native boats leave the main island (Sangihe), rowing in their direction. The native boats were approximately two miles away when the pilots sighted a Catalina flying along the northern coast of Sangihe. The Catalina scared the native boats back toward shore. The Catalina then turned around just before reaching the spot where the two P-51s were ditched, flew back along the coast and turned north, flying along the east coast of Manipal and Boakide Islands, and continued on north. The pilots were now about three miles from the shore. The Catalina evidently did not see them, even though they waved and Lt. Finch fired his .45 twice in the direction of the PBY. It then seemed that all hope was gone, but they decided to make the best of the situation. At that time, a slight rain passed over, and, laying with their mouths open, the two pilots were able to get enough water to wet their throats and lips, which by now were very dry and starting to crack. They then sighted a small buoy sticking out of the water just north of Manipal Island, and decided to row to that spot by nightfall.

At approximately 1230/I, when the pilots were about one and a half miles off Manipal, they sighted seven native boats put out from Manipal. These boats were carrying both natives and unarmed Japs. The boats surrounded the two pilots. The pilots surmised that some of the occupants were unmistakably Japs because they wore short khaki pants, two of them had white civilian hats, and a few had perfectly trimmed mustaches. The hair of most of them was straight, rather long, and appeared to be combed. Most of them had yellowish-white skin, and none of them were a dark as the natives the pilots had seen before in the Netherland East Indies; and they had more intelligent faces. The pilots discussed the possibility of their being Jap civilians sent to populate the island.

With Lt. Finch displaying his .45 prominently, the two pilots by sign language asked the occupants to bring them food and coconuts. Since it seemed a hopeless situation, they were ready to try anything. The natives made signs for the two pilots to get into the native boats and go with them where they would secure food and water for them. However, Lts. Finch and Woliung decided that they weren't that hungry. They were also determined not to be taken alive. They decided to row out to sea as far as possible, thinking that they might possibly discourage the Japs and natives from following them. The native boats proceeded to surround the two pilots in their rubber rafts, in order to block their pass. One Jap (wearing khaki shorts and no shirt) in a boat by himself began to try to persuade the other to attack Lts. Finch and Woliung. Part of his talk contained English and the two pilots could make out the phrases "make lots of money" and "turn over to Jap policeman". Several of the natives answered him and the word "pistol" could be distinguished in each one's speech. He had been talking to them for quite some time, and they began to act as if they were getting ready to attack. They kept edging closer to the pilots' rafts, and were grinning in a most disturbing manner. At this time, 1330, the two pilots heard planes and, looking up, saw two Spitfires rounding Manipal Island and turning toward them. They passed overhead and the native boats scattered. The Spitfires buzzed twice and then one left to get help, and the other kept circling the two pilots. While he was circling, one of the native boats, containing 14 men, started coming toward the pilots. The Spitfire buzzed them, causing them to jump overboard. They righted the boat and returned to shore. When another boat with four men started toward the pilots a little later, the Spitfire fired across the bow of the native boat, causing them to jump overboard also. As the native boats were returning to shore, the Spitfire made another pass firing behind them, speeding them on their way. The Spitfire then had to leave because his gas supply required him to return to base. In the 10 minutes which elapsed before a Catalina arrived, four native boats put out to sea again, but turned back when the Catalina came in sight. The Catalina picked up Lts. Finch and Woliung at 1430 and, after taking off, went to the spot where the P-51s had been ditched and made three strafing passes, getting in good hits. The Catalina then took them home. On the Catalina, they were fed pork chops, boned turkey, and fruit cocktail.

They were give first aid for sunburn and scratches upon the hands. Lt. Woliung's feet were treated for cuts and bruises because the night before he had taken his shoes off on the beach and was forced to run into the water over the rough coral, with his shoes in his hand.

They were left at the 13th Emergency Air-Sea Rescue Squadron camp, where they ate another meal and were given liquor; and from there they were taken to the 2nd Field Hospital, where they spent the night.

After receiving clean clothes from the hospital, they left via C-46 at 1100 on 9 June, landing at Dulag at 1315/I. The pilots caught another C-46, which took off from Dulag and landed with Lts. Finch and Woliung at Clark Field at 1730.

17

DITCHING AN A-20

Submitted by: Captain E. L. Davidson Jr., A-20 Pilot, 84 Missions, 228 Hours, New Guinea and surrounding Islands, 417thBomb Group, 675thBomb Squadron (L), 5thAir Force

I was the formation leader of a flight of six A-20s with the target assigned as Ambon Bay. Our attack was made in two three-ship elements at minimum altitude, strafing and bombing. Our bomb load was four 500 pounders. We hit immediate target, shipping at Ambon Town. My bomb run was at minimum altitude and as I dropped two bombs on luggers in the bay, I received a burst of medium caliber ack/ack fire in the rear fuselage. As I dropped my third bomb, two ack/ack bursts were received. One damaged the upper left section of my instrument panel, the other knocked out my left engine, destroying the upper cowling of my left engine and damaging the leading edge of my left wing. I immediately feathered the left prop and cut switches and gas to the left engine, closed the left cowl flaps and lowered 10 degrees the landing flaps. I dropped my last bomb, then closed the bomb bay doors. As I was trimming the aircraft for straight and level flying on the single engine, the left engine and left wing caught fire. I called my gunner and ordered him to prepare for ditching; the gunner replied that he could not; I presume he was wounded by the ack/ack fire.

The aircraft was burning fiercely when I lowered the flaps and made a normal water landing in Ambon Bay. My safety harness was fastened and properly adjusted before takeoff and I wish to emphasize the great impor-tance of this safety precaution. The airplane skidded on the surface, one or two times, to the best of my knowledge, before making an initial and final impact. The nose section was crushed back into the cockpit to the extent that the rudder pedals were forced back to my seat. Slight bruises on my feet and legs were my only injury.

Both wings of the aircraft were broken off when it hit the water and the cockpit was submerged instantly. I pulled the canopy emergency release, which failed, but the regular release handle opened the canopy. The safety harness was released and I emerged from the cockpit with my parachute on, and grabbed the raft release and it immediately came to the surface. It was not necessary for me to inflate my life vest because the parachute held me up. As I pulled the raft free from the sinking aircraft I observed the tail sec-tion was broken at the position in back of the gunner's compartment. The aircraft completely submerged within a few seconds, I would estimate about twelve seconds. I did not see any trace of my gunner. I experienced some difficulty in inflating my life raft because I could not locate the bottle or the string. I suggest each crew member be thoroughly familiar with the raft in any airplane he flies, such as the manner in which it is folded, the contents and the exact location of contents. After inflation of raft I paddled seaward as rapidly as possible. I was continuously fired upon from shore installa-tions, by light and medium explosives, but the rough sea prevented accu-racy.

Another plane in the flight, piloted by Lt. Mitchell, circled and guarded my location for forty-five minutes, under intense enemy ack/ack fire. He made radio contact with Rescue Catalina, giving Fighter Grid position. The Catalina answered that they were low on fuel but that they would proceed immediately. Lt. Mitchell circled until 1500/I which was as long as he pos-sibly could, due to lack of fuel. I paddled until 1600/I and was two or three miles at sea from the mouth of Ambon Bay when I first heard and saw the Rescue Catalina approaching from the east. The Catalina came within a mile of me and then turned right to search the mouth of the Bay and the coast and even ventured into the Bay in spite of intense ack/ack. He made two passes but could not locate me either time due to the clouds and haze. On the third pass the sun came from behind a cloud allowing me to signal him with my mirror. I later learned that was to be the final pass and my signal with the mirror was the only thing that caught the pilot's attention. Needless to say, I cannot over emphasize the importance of crew members being thoroughly familiar with the use of the signal mirror.

I boarded the Catalina at 1625 and the crew sank my life raft. After moving to the interior of the aircraft I saw machine gun tracers and spouts under the left wing but could not see the enemy aircraft that made the pass. The pilot headed into the weather and took off and upon leaving the water I heard more gunfire and saw more tracers pass the aircraft. The pilot used excellent evasive action and escaped into the clouds after the third and final pass by the enemy aircraft. All passes were made from the sun and only a faint sighting was made, not sufficient to establish identification. The enemy pilot broke away high from his attacks and fire was inaccurate. The Catalina pilot kept constant position reports during the return flight and we landed there at 1730/I with five minutes' fuel.

This was my second ditching and I was confident the Catalina Rescue boat would be there. I was only hoping it would arrive before dark. The courageous performance of duty on the part of the rescue crew with utter disregard to their own personal safety is typical of their performance in the theater and they should receive high commendation for their excellent work.

Situation Date: 22 October 1944

EPILOGUE

The Douglas A-20 Havoc was an agile, twin-engine attack bomber that saw extensive combat in the Pacific. In this story, it was at the epicenter of intense combat. The two-man bomber was shot down; then the Catalina came under fire. The impact with the ocean literally destroyed the A-20 and nearly killed the pilot. The gunner did not survive.

18

ONE MAN'S DAY

The following third-person report was filed on behalf of the crewman involved.

****

Lt. B, flying a P-51D, was on a B-29 escort mission to Osaka. Two and one-half hours from base the squadron ran into some haze and fog, with visibility about one mile. Later, it encountered an extremely turbulent front too high to fly over. Weather had forecast a front at about his area, but not of this intensity or reaching above 10,000 feet. Shortly after penetrating the front, Lt. B's engine started cutting out, due, he believes, to icing in the carburetor. He lost sight of the rest of the flight. The flight leader was circling, attempting to keep in radio contact with the navigator B-29 and the rest of the flight. Lt. B went down to 3,000 feet and then 500 feet, still in the weather, and tried repeatedly to raise the flight leader and the navigator B-29 without success. Later he was sure his transmitter was out.

With his engine kicking up, he took a reciprocal heading toward base and came out of the weather. His engine was functioning all right for the moment and he climbed back to about 9,000 feet and tried to get a heading from base, but got no answer. At approximately 1100 hours, one hour after he had started on his return flight, his engine started sputtering again. Lt. B went into full rich, turned on his IFF and transmitted his location (approx. 250 mi. NW of Iwo Jima) which, of course, was not received, as his transmitter was not functioning. He lost altitude rapidly. At 2,000 feet, with fuel pressure way down, he banked and turned left, jettisoned his canopy, and dived out over the side past the left wing. His chute opened immediately and he had no trouble on the way down. He tried unsuccessfully to unfasten his leg straps before dunking. As soon as he was in the water he unsnapped his chest and leg strap fasteners without too much trouble. He was able to keep away from his chute enough not to get tangled in it, except for two shroud lines which he found caught to him after he had inflated his Mae West and raft, and had climbed in. (Lt. B had some trouble locating the CO_2 bottle at first—being heavy, it tends to sink to the bottom side when the raft is pulled loose from the raft pack.) He cut these two lines loose and kept them, but the rest of the chute floated out of reach.

B-29s passed over on their return from target, and Lt. B fired flares but was not able to attract their attention. Later in the day, the fog closed in and he heard what sounded like a PBY circling in the area, but he was never able to see it. On the third day a B-29 mission passed overhead, one by one, and Lt. B broke out sea markers, fired flares, used smoke bombs, and fired tracer ammunition without attracting anyone's attention.

On the fifth day, towards evening, the sea started to get rougher and by midnight a grade A typhoon was shaping up. Lt. B kept well covered with a poncho and hood; he found the hood leaked some, but by raising the poncho with his knees was able to keep a lot of sea water running off the raft rather that into it. However, there was still plenty of water in the raft—it never was completely dry the whole six days. During the night he was upset five times—not by swells, which were running very high, but which the raft rode well—but by the white caps on top of the waves which broke under the raft and tipped it over.

Twice Lt. B climbed back into the raft, pulling his back pack with him. The third time he used the parachute shrouds—he tied them to the back pack and the raft pack and hung them over the side. That was all right, except that during the night, the back pack disappeared with everything in it —his pistol, knife, most of his food and water and his desalination water kit. A large fish may have been attracted by the bright white line and snapped it, or in the very rough going, the weight of the back pack jerking on the end of the line may have snapped it.

Toward evening of the sixth day afloat, Lt. B started hearing things. That night he carried on a completely imaginary but very plausible conversation with the Iwo tower, telling them where he was and for ———'s sake to get a boat out to him. The answer was—"Hold onto your shirt, we'll get someone there to pick you up. You're O.K." In the morning he heard music and then imaginary voices on an imaginary destroyer which was standing by to rescue him. He whistled, talked with some of his squadron mates, and everything was dandy. He was still balmy when a life guard sub, almost two miles away, happened to be on the crest of a swell at the same moment the raft was on the crest of another, and spotted him.

Still under the illusion he'd been talking to the tower and to a destroyer, Lt. B was not a bit surprised when he glanced over his shoulder and saw a sub making for him. The sub missed him on the first pass, but with some difficulty got next to him on the second. Much to the surprise of the crew of the sub, Lt. B stepped aboard and calmly announced he's been talking to the tower at Iwo and had been waiting for them—what had held them up so long? The position was approximately half way between Iwo and Japan.

SURVIVAL DATA

1. *Equipment.* Lt. B, with his para-raft pack, knife, pistol, water proof holster, cloth chart, and back pack, was about as well equipped as anyone could be in a one-man raft.

2. *Food.* Included in his para-raft pack and back pack were two cans of pemmican, and in his pockets he had two small bars of chocolate. Actually he was never particularly conscious of hunger, and ate only three-quarters of one of the rations. Of course he lost the rest of this food rations when he and his back pack parted company on the fifth night. If Lt. B had been without food, he had two good opportunities of obtaining it. On the sixth night a friendly bird about the size of a pigeon, with a dark back, a white spot on its head, a lighter belly and a straight beak (possibly a noody or sooty tern) alighted on his raft and kept him company all night. Once he left the raft to grab a small fish, and that could have been two sources of food, plus blood for liquid.

3. From time to time Lt. B also saw small fish, four to six inches long, with blue and black stripes (possibly small bonita) around the raft. There

undoubtedly were other fish enjoying the shade under the raft in the day time—good food and good bait, which could have been caught with the net which was part of the back pack kit.

4. *Water.* Drinking water was no problem until after Lt. B had lost his back pack. He had three pint cans of water, and the Permutit kit. If he had needed it, he could have caught rain water in his poncho or sea anchor. Actually, he did not drink any.

EPILOGUE

Large groups of B-29s flew in formations clustered around a lead plane with the lead navigator. This extra crewman was not carried in all of the bombers. The P-51 Mustangs were escorts. This Mustang pilot was lucky. He ditched in the open seas, alone, and was adrift for six days. He was picked up by a submarine just as he was losing his mind. President George H. W. Bush was likewise rescued in this manner, as were a total of 520 downed aviators.

Pemmican is a mixture of meat and fat dried out in cakes about the size of classroom erasers. It goes back hundreds of years as basic nourishment for soldiers. The Permutit is a desalinization kit sold to the Navy by the Permutit Company.

19

THE AMERICAN COASTWATCHERS

The following third-person report was filed on behalf of the crewmen involved.

****

5 November 1944

At 0630 on 5 November the USS *Intrepid* launched an attack group of VT, VB and VF at a point approximately 150 miles north of Legaspi Peninsula, Luzon, to conduct a bombing and strafing attack on Legaspi Airfield. Lt. Demoss participated in this fight of the escorting fighters flying in the division led by Lt. Brownell. The weather was poor, and as the group approached the target the VF and VB lost sight of the VT. The VFs began escorting the VBs in their diving attack and, finding no air opposition, they started strafing attacks on the Field. Brownells's division made three strafing runs, pulling out somewhere between 50 and 100 feet, and succeeded in burning a parked air plane. Nothing but small caliber AA was encountered and Demoss did not realize until later that his plane had been hit during the attack. He found out ten minutes later when the group was cruising around over Legaspi Gulf, trying to join up, and suddenly his oil pressure began to drop off sharply. He told Brownell about it and they immediately started for home together. About ten minutes later, when they were about northeast of

San Miguel Point, still over Legaspi Gulf, the oil pressure dropped to zero and his prop went into full low pitch.

Demoss, then flying at 3,000 feet, immediately started to get ready to ditch. In addition to the usual precautions such as tightening shoulder straps, locking open-pit enclosure, lowering the seat, etc., he took out his pocket knife and cut his parachute free from his harness and life raft so that he could remove the essential items from the plane without being encumbered by the parachute, which he did not thing he would need. One thing he forgot to do was to jettison his belly tank, an omission which fortunately caused no damage. He then made a full flap, full stall, landing in the sheltered waters of the Gulf. There was practically no wind and the water was glass. The landing was no rougher than a sloppy carrier landing and the belly tank ripped immediately with no disastrous effect.

Demoss climbed out on the wing and lifted out his harness and survival gear that he had unbuckled prior to landing. Meanwhile, his division leader circled him very low with full flaps and watched to see that he got squared away with his life raft. Demoss did not succeed in doing so as the inflating mechanism failed to function. He was unable to get at the tube in order to blow up the raft because of the fact that a small rag which was tied over the end of the tube was knotted too tightly after becoming wet and became very difficult to untie. In the struggle he was forced to let go of his back pack in order to save the raft, and in the end he had to abandon the raft to keep from being dragged under. On seeing this, Brownell extracted his own raft from the seat pack and dropped it to Demoss. It was a very good drop, only yards away, and Demoss had no trouble in getting to the raft and inflating it. It contained a can of water, two cans of sea marker, a medical kit and a desalinization kit. In addition, Demoss had on his person his life jacket, gun, a pocket flashlight and a package of dye marker. He was wearing a summer flying suit, Marine issue. He also had a RAAF silk map of Luzon.

Brownell took departure soon thereafter, and Demoss began paddling in order to maintain his position in the hope of being rescued later by an OS2U. He paddled all day long and by 1700 was still in approximately the same position. During this time he saw no more planes. It turned out that the Task Force had moved on to attack other objectives. When darkness fell it was raining hard and the wind was increasing. It was so dark that Demoss could not tell where he was drifting. The winds increased steadily and Demoss had a most uncomfortable night, suffering from seasickness. At one point he took a small shot of morphine to make himself more comfortable, and under its influence he managed to get a little sleep.

The following morning it was still raining and blowing. Demoss found himself about a half a mile off Bataan Island. He saw a sandy beach a little way up and paddled through the heavy surf in order to reach it. Shortly after he got there a small "banca" sailed in close to the beach, and the crew of four Filipinos looked at him somewhat dubiously, apparently wondering whether he was Jap or American. After much frantic waving and yelling on Demoss's part, they brought the boat ashore and Demoss introduced himself. All four of the Filipinos, who were fishermen, spoke some English, and Demoss had no trouble making himself understood. In fact, Demoss said that the entire time he was on Luzon he never encounter any Filipinos who couldn't speak at least a little English. The fishermen were quite anxious to leave as there were Japs in the vicinity. They took him to a small barrio in which was their home. There he was fed some chicken, chicken broth and rice and given a bed to sleep in, for he was still very seasick. He spent most of the day sleeping only to find that the fishermen had washed his clothes for him.

That evening a guerrilla lieutenant from the forces of Major Flor arrived at the house and identified himself to Demoss with a somewhat incomprehensible note. The natives vouched for him, and Demoss decided to accompany him to Major Flor's camp. Two of them sailed all that night in another banca, arriving the following morning at the guerrilla camp on the shore of Cagraray Island. There he was welcomed by Major Flor, a Filipino officer, formerly of the Philippine Army, and was invited to stay with the Major and his wife in a small house about a half a mile inland. Major Flor commanded about 200 men, plus a group of 700 or more "reserves" who had some training from his men. His arms consisted of about 50 Enfield rifles, a few grenades, and one highly prized Thompson machine gun which was almost out of ammunition. The guerrilla force had been quite active during the past year, ambushing Jap convoys, wrecking trains; they had successfully wrecked two trains loaded with Jap troops on one occasion, assisting in the escape of a number of American internees and some local women from a work detail at Naga. Some of them were present in Flor's camp and others were scattered in various places, hiding with natives. At this time there was a large number of Japs in the Legaspi area, many of them engaged in hastily erected defenses against a possible invasion. Major Flor's outfit collected a great deal of intelligence about their activities, supplemented by excellent maps, and this material was later transmitted by Demoss to our forces on Leyte. (Major Flor had no radio transmitter, only a Zenith battery receiver with which they listened to American newscasts.)

Two days after he had arrived, three more American airmen appeared on the scene. They were Lt. (jg) Keene, a VT pilot from the *Hancock,* and his two crewmen, Taylor and Dickerson, who had been forced down near Catanduanes and rescued by the guerrilla forces of Major Torso. Their reception by Flor was by no means as cordial as Demoss's had been, and he soon learned that there was a good deal of rivalry and ill feeling between Flor and Torso, a situation that is not unusual among Filipino guerrilla bands. Apparently a messenger sent by Flor to Torso some time before had been completely stripped and disarmed by Torso's men and sent packing, and the incident still rankled.

It was decided to send the four Americans to Samar, which, it was believed as a result of exuberant news broadcasts, was entirely in our hands. It was later discovered that many areas on Samar, including one at which they had intended to land, were still very much in enemy hands. During the four or five days that Demoss spent with Flor, two sailboats were gotten ready for the voyage, and in the meantime Demoss lived very comfortably in the Major's house. A dance was held in honor of the Americans, and a number of girls, many of them not unattractive, were brought over from Legaspi especially for the occasion.

When the boats were ready, the four American set out, Keene and his men along with two of Torso's representatives in one boat, and Demoss and two of Flor's men in the other. After four days of sailing, during which they occasionally put in for food or sleep at small barrios, the boats put in at a little village about 10 miles north of Matnog, in Sorsogon Province, Legaspi, where it was hoped they would find Sergeant Becker, an American coastwatcher who had a radio. Becker was there, and also another American, Lt. Chapman, both of the U.S. Army. Chapman has been in the Philippines ever since the start of the war, and in that time has been on almost every island. He is presently engaged in intelligence work for the Southwest Pacific forces and has a radio of his own, in addition to Becker's. Becker was put ashore on Luzon by a submarine to collect and transmit weather data and to act as coastwatcher. Becker and Chapman operate alone, shifting their location frequently and keeping about one jump ahead of the Japs, who are quite aware of their presence on the island. They were at that time extremely low on provisions of all sorts. Becker was dressed in rags, and had no shoes, only a few drugs and a little Philippine pre-invasion currency. He existed chiefly on rice, which he purchased in small quantities from the poverty-stricken Filipinos. While they were with Becker and Chapman, the pilots, hungry for fresh meat, succeeded in convincing a local farmer to sell them a young heifer in return for a note stating that the U.S. Navy would pay the bill. Demoss hopes that the Navy in due course will honor the debt. The heifer was butchered by Taylor, an expert, and was delicious.

Becker sent a radio message to our forces at Leyte giving the names of the four survivors and requesting that a PT boat or Dumbo be sent to evacuate them. The message was receipted for but not answered, and no Dumbo or PT put in an appearance.

By this time both of the pilots were in very poor shape. Demoss had had touches of dysentery (he could have used halazone to good advantage, but had none) and had developed an unidentified tropical fever. Keene had cut his knee badly while hacking at something with a knife and the wound had become badly infected. He was showing symptoms of blood poisoning. Becker had some sulfa drugs with which he treated both Demoss and Keene, probably saving the latter's life.

After two and a half days a message was finally received from our forces instructing the airmen to sail to Oras on Samar Island. This trip was impracticable to attempt in a small sailboat as it involved sailing upwind in unprotected seas for quite a long distance, so it was determined to try to reach our forces at some other point on Samar, preferably Capalonga, which had been reported in news broadcasts as being in American hands—falsely as it turned out.

On the day this message arrived, Colonel Escadero, the leader of a large guerrilla force controlling most of southern Sogorson, appeared on the scene and announced to the Americans that they were now in his custody and protection since he was in control of the area. He stated that he would take charge of transporting the Americans to Leyte. Demoss and Keene declined politely, saying that they were already being well taken care of by Becker, and at this Escadero became more insistent, and slightly threatening. Demoss became a little angry and told Escadero quite firmly that they had no intention of going with him. By this time all hands were nervously fingering their firearms and the situation was distinctly tense. Escadero finally backed down, however, and retired with his bodyguard of 8 or 10 guerrillas.

Demoss learned that Escadero, a full-blooded Spaniard of approximately 65, had reacted quite actively to the recent landing on Leyte and had taken the occasion to have his forces blow up a number of bridges, cut all the telephone wires in the area, and kill a considerable number of Japs. As a result, his forces were now very low on ammunition and were encountering some difficulty from the highly incensed Japs. Another of Escadero's activities was stealing gasoline from the Japs, which he turned over to Becker for use in the engine with which Becker charged his batteries.

As one of the sailboats had become badly damaged, the party embarked on the final stage of their journey in the other banca. Becker came along for part of the journey as a sort of bodyguard, bringing a machine gun with him. The party consisted of the four American airmen, Becker, two of Flor's men, and the three man crew of the banca, a very heavy load for the little boat. The two escorts from Major Torso's forces were left behind for lack of space.

After a precarious trip across San Bernardino Strait, the party put in at a barrio near the northern tip of Samar which was known to be friendly. There they learned that there were many Japs at Capalonga and that it was by no means a safe place to land, as they had hitherto believed. They spend the night at the barrio. Keene passed out from exhaustion after walking a short distance from the shore to the house where they were to sleep and Demoss became seriously worried about him. The next day, however, he seemed better, and the party sent out again, this time without Becker, who had decided to return to his job on Samar and had departed in another boat.

They sailed between Allen and St Anton Islands and down along the western coast of Samar, stopping off from time to time for food and rest at barrios known to be safe. At midnight of the second night they put in at the town of Zumarrage, on Buad Island, and here they met the first U. S. patrol. It was a ten man anti-malaria unit engaged in spraying the area with insecticide. The LCMs which had brought the patrol up there had not yet departed to return to Leyte but were remaining all night. The next day Demoss and party were taken to Tacloban on the LCMs. The guerrilla representatives came along as they were hoping to obtain arms, or a promise of future delivery of arms, and had also undertaken to get some supplies for Becker. One of the guerrilla representatives, Major Flor's brother, had been a Chief Machinist's Mate stationed at Cavite when the war broke out. He was coming to Leyte in the hope of signing back into the Navy. Demoss is not sure whether he succeeded in doing so but presumes that he was able to join up again without difficulty.

At Tacloban, Demoss made out a list of the various supplies that Becker needed and gave it to an ACI officer named Ross who promised to do his best to see that Becker's needs were filled and also to see that the other guerrilla officer was assisted in his attempt to get arms for Major Flor.

On the evening of the day he arrived, Demoss went aboard the Currituck, which took him to Hollandia.

20

THE SLOT

When pilots flew northwest from up into the Solomons from Guadalcanal, they threaded a series of islands and they called it "the slot".

CHOISEUL NATIVES TAKE CARE OF TWO PILOTS AND TWO GUNNERS

The following third-person report was filed on behalf of the crewmen involved.

****

Ensign Hollandsworth took off in his TBF on February 4th with a striking force to attack 20 Jap destroyers coming down the slot. The Japs' task force was contacted 200 miles from Guadalcanal on bearing 300°T at 1610. Hollandsworth was at 12,000 feet when a burst of an AA shell threw fragments into the engine, causing it to sputter, and the plane began to lose altitude; so Hollandsworth radioed that he was going down. The message was picked up and subsequently reported by Lt. Comdr. Brunton, the leader of the section. Just after he sent the message, Hollandsworth's motor conked out, and he headed for the coast of Choiseul Island with no power. The Zeros took chase. Pilot Hollandsworth jettisoned the torpedo at high speed, circling off near the water for the subsequent landing.

There were four Zeros (square tips) on his tail making overhead passes from the starboard out of the sun with pullout overhead on the same side to return from another pass. Ensign Hollandsworth twisted and turned to avoid Zeros' fire. One Zero tried to come up from below, and Radio Gunner Adcock let loose with the .30 cal., hitting the engine of the Zero, causing it to leave the attack smoking, but it was not seen to fall. The first Zero attacking hit the turret, putting it out of commission. Radio Gunner Adcock received a shrapnel wound in his leg but the others were unscratched.

Hollandsworth made a good landing with wheels up and flaps down, pancaking into the water, touching tail first. Just before the landing, he told Adcock to open the escape door, and upon stopping in the water all three men got out of the plane without difficulty. Plane intercommunications were satisfactory up to the end, in spite of the engine being cut out. The two Zeros started strafing, and Hollandsworth and Adcock got under the wing, but Walker was out to the side about 5 feet. The Zeros concentrated on Walker, and he was hit and went under and was not seen again. The plane sank just about that time, but Hollandsworth had already pulled out the life raft and first-aid packet.

About a half hour later the rubber boat was inflated and Hollandsworth and Adcock started paddling for shore two or three miles away. Halfway there they were picked up by natives in a canoe and taken to their small village on the southeastern part of Choiseul Island. The natives there could understand English and one could speak it. The crew of an SBD, Lt. Murphy and Radio Gunner Williamson, came to this village, having been picked up by the natives also. Lt. Murphy took care of Adcock's wound.

The two crews stayed in the village until February 8th, being well treated and receiving everything they asked for, if available. Sweet potatoes, coconuts, pineapple and papaya were the main food. A Methodist mission had been there previously and educated the natives, but most of the natives on Choiseul were secretive at all times. Our men lay around until a strange native arrived on February 6th and said that he could take the men to the white man (coast watcher). Plans were made to leave the next night, but it rained; so it was postponed until the night of February 8th. Murphy and Hollandsworth left, leaving Adcock and Williamson behind in the village.

Travel was at night, and the first leg was in a canoe manned by 14 natives. One stop was made and all rested. The crew was changed, then they went on. The next leg was 15 miles on foot with the going pretty tough. The party stopped at another village, and then another canoe ride. The whole trip seemed to be planned in every detail. A stop was made, and the coast watcher sent a note stating that the deal was not phony. Then there was a steep climb through jungle and swamps taking 5 hours. The pilots were well received and the C.W. promptly radioed in the details to Guadalcanal, receiving a reply that all four would be picked up on February 12th. The PBY arrived as scheduled and the party of four returned at noon of the 12th of February to Guadalcanal.

21

CARRIER PILOT DOWN

The following third-person report was filed on behalf of the crewman involved.

****

19 December 1944.

Ens. Crittenden took off at 0450 on 28 October 44 together with 16 other F6Fs for a patrol mission over Leyte. At this time the *Enterprise* was 160 mile east of Leyte. The plane that Crittenden was flying had been shot up pretty badly two days previously during a strike on Clark Field, but damaged equipment had been replaced and two .30 cal. holes in the left wing tank had been patched.

The patrol flown was on a line running north and south ten miles east of Ormoc, and the purpose was to protect ground operations and Allied ships from Japanese planes. The patrol was to be flown at 20,000 feet but soon after arriving on station the patrol was ordered down to 18,000 feet to intercept some bogies that had been reported at that altitude. The patrol dropped down to 10,000 feet during the run from north to south but no enemy planes were spotted. Just as Crittenden was making his turn to the north his left wing tank exploded. He had not seen any tracers, but learned later from others in his flight that a "Jack" had hit him.

The explosion blew into the cockpit, and even though Crittenden opened his cockpit enclosure immediately and bailed out, he was severely burned on his legs, arms and face. His coveralls and helmet were burned off completely and his face was so badly burned that one of his eyes was swollen shut completely and the other was just a narrow slit. He encountered no difficulty in getting out of the plane, but he opened his chute too quickly because he believed he had been unconscious and had fallen a long distance. The wind was blowing from the southeast so Crittenden was carried out over Ormoc Bay, where he landed in the water. He managed to get all but one buckle of his harness undone before he hit the water, and he undid the last one as soon as he hit. He inflated one side of his Mae West and then got out his paracraft and inflated that and climbed in. All of the equipment was missing from the raft and he doesn't know whether he lost it in getting his raft out or whether it had never been in it.

The wind on the water was blowing from the southwest and Crittenden noticed that he was being blown right toward Ormoc. About one half hour after getting in his raft he was approached by some small outrigger sailboats coming from the west. One of these came to within about fifty feet but would approach no further until Crittenden waved and yelled, "Filipino." The natives in the canoe then yelled "Americano" and came in and picked him up together with all his equipment. It wasn't until he got in the canoe that he realized that he still had his back-pack strapped to him.

One native in the canoe spoke English but the other one didn't. The load proved too heavy for this canoe as water kept coming over the side, so one of the other canoes came alongside and Crittenden was transferred so that his equipment was in one canoe and he was in the other. They then made for shore and landed on the west coast of Ormoc Bay. The boats had been sent out to pick up Crittenden by an organization known as the Volunteer Guards, which is a civilian organization that arms themselves with bolo knives.

As soon as they reached shore, Crittenden was turned over to Sgt. Astoria Valiea, who was in the 90th Infantry Regiment of the 3rd Battalion of Company L, a guerrilla organization. The commanding officer of Company L is Lt. Apolonia.

The Japs had evidently seen Crittenden land as they sent patrols out after him from the north and south but the guerrillas were able to kill off these patrols before they could get in to Crittenden. One patrol of 30 Japs was chased along the beach by the guerrillas, who would not waste their previous ammunition on them, but who used their bolo knives instead. One Jap ran out into the ocean and the guerrilla who was chasing him put his bolo knife in his teeth and swam out after him. He returned a few minutes later with the Jap hanging by his neck on the bolo knife which had been cleanly inserted from fore to aft. The guerrilla presented the Jap to Crittenden, who was in too bad shape himself to show his true gratitude.

The guerrillas sent for a doctor immediately but he was at Matlano (across the peninsula) and it took the doctor quite some time to get there. When he arrived it was found that he had nothing with which to treat burns, so he gave Crittenden a shot of morphine and sent a messenger to La Pox (on the eastern side of Leyte) where it was known that there was a supply of boric acid ointment. It took the messenger five days to make the trip and he got shot by a Jap in the process, but he finally returned with the ointment. Crittenden was in a coma off and on from 28 October until 2 November, when he awoke to find himself in Matlano. He discovered later that the Japs had sent a strong force to get him and the guerrillas had carried him on a litter to Matlano. It was at Matlano at the Battalion Aid Station that his burns were finally treated with the boric acid ointment.

Crittenden had to remain in bed during the next 20 days and he said that the Japs must have been tipped off that he had gone to Matlano as they strafed and bombed that village every night. Fortunately the Battalion Aid Station was back in the hills from the village so it wasn't hit.

Crittenden began to walk a little on 22 November and gradually was able to get his strength back. He couldn't speak highly enough of the wonderful treatment accorded him by all of the natives and guerrillas. They gave him the best food available (chicken and eggs) and also supplied him with a pair of Jap khaki trousers and cigarettes that had been taken from the Japs.

Around the first of December, Crittenden was joined by four Army pilots that had been shot down. After an unsuccessful attempt by a PT boat to pick Crittenden up at Matlano (Japs prevented the PT from getting in), Crittenden and his four Army companions decided to try to make it through the Jap lines, with the help of guerrillas, to Abijao, on the west coast of Leyte, where the guerrilla headquarters were located. They travelled north to a little village west of Ormoc where they received word that two

PBYs had landed at Matlano to pick them up. In the meantime, survivors from the USS *Cooper* had come ashore at Matlano, so the PBYs took those survivors off. (One PBY took off with 66 survivors in addition to its crew of six.) The PBYs had been instructed to return five days later to pick up Crittenden and the four Army pilots, so when Crittenden got this news, he and his companions headed back for Matlano, where they arrived on the night of 9 December 44.

On 10 December 44 an Army PBY landed at Matlano and took Crittenden and the four Army pilots aboard. They took off and landed on the strip at Tacloban at 1300 on 10 December. The four Army pilots were left there and Crittenden had expected to go on immediately to a seaplane tender anchored in San Pedro Bay. The PBY was sent on another mission, however, and returned at 1500, when it took Crittenden aboard and flew him out to the USS *Orca* (AVP). There they outfitted Crittenden as well as possible and returned him to Hawaii by way of Palau and Guam. Crittenden arrived in Hawaii 16 December 44.

Crittenden says that the Filipinos are rabidly pro-American and can't do enough to help an American survivor in any way possible. They are in desperate need of medical supplies, arms and clothing. Guerrillas are fairly well clothed and fed as they kill Jap landing parties and take their food, clothing and arms. Some of the better class native are still reasonably well-clothed, although none of them have shoes. The poorer classes are desperate for want of clothing.

Even though the Japs supposedly control the coastline around Ormoc Bay, the guerrillas are very active there and move about at will. The Japanese are scared to death of the guerrillas.

Crittenden did not wear GI shoes because he said they were too uncomfortable. He wore regular low-quarter shoes, but fortunately he didn't have to do much walking because of his condition.

He had forgotten his gun when he took off from the carrier, and although he didn't need it, he wished that he had had it so that he could have given it to the guerrillas.

Ordinarily Crittenden didn't wear his back-pack because it was too uncomfortable but he happened to take it with him on this trip and he says he couldn't have gotten along without it. He lived on his malted milk tablets for the first three days as he was unable to keep even soup in his stomach. He used all his morphine syrettes as the pain from his burns was unbearable. He used his iodine to purify some native water, although he heard from the doctor that all the water in that area was safe to drink. He drank all of the water in his back-pack when he first got ashore. Everything in his back-pack was valuable to him but he would like to have double the amount of medical supplies the next time he goes out.

Crittenden had no trouble in operating any of his equipment, and no complaints other than the lack of equipment in his raft.

22

EVASION IN ENEMY WATERS

The following report is Sgt. Rocco's account of his experiences when he and his crew were forced to ditch the B-25 and spend three days at sea. They were picked up and returned to our forces through Filipino guerrillas.

It was the 28th of November, and we were attacking a Jap task force in the vicinity of Leyte. To ensure maximum accuracy, we had lowered our bombing altitude to about 300 feet in spite of heavy enemy anti-aircraft opposition. The first I knew of the emergency was when the pilot shouted over the interphone, "We're hit and on fire; going down." I glanced out of the waist window and noticed that our gear had evidently been shot up and was hanging down. Our speed, the pilot told us later, was in excess of 200 miles an hour. We pulled off the bomb run and started going down in a gradual glide, when two of the men lost their head and jumped out of the ship from an altitude of approximately 100 feet. It is presumed that they were both killed instantly, since we never saw either of them again. This incident serves to illustrate the necessity for air discipline and training in ditching procedure. Our crew had received the usual amount of training in ditching the aircraft, and it was thought prior to this time that our air discipline was pretty good. A few seconds after the men jumped out, we hit. The first impact was terrific and threw me against the bulkhead with some force. Contrary to what we had been led to believe, the second impact was much less severe than the first. What happened between the time we hit and when we found ourselves out of the plane and in the water is not at all clear in my mind. The navigator was killed; and after the plane had stopped moving, I found myself in the water with the pilot and another crew member and the raft. The plane broke in two and sank in about thirty seconds after it had lost its forward momentum.

The three of us boarded the raft and secured all emergency equipment we had to the sides of the raft. A Jap destroyer of the task force which we were attacking had swung out of line and was bearing down on us, evidently with the intention of picking us up and taking us prisoner. However, before it could reach us, two P-47s of our fighter cover intercepted it and drove it off.

The first night out nothing happened. It was too dark for us to figure our location, although we knew we were within a few miles of Leyte Bay. When dawn broke the next morning it was raining, and we attempted to catch sea rain water in the rubber buckets provided in the emergency equipment for this purpose. Using these we were able to catch several pints of water. We drank quite a lot of this water, and the rest was lost since the rubber buckets leaked pretty badly.

At about 10:00 in the morning of the second day a single-engine Jap plane was seen approaching our position. The pilot directed us to all get out of the raft and turn it over so that the blue underside would camouflage our position. The raft itself would have been quite easy to turn over and handle had it not been for the fact that the auxiliary equipment tied to the sides of the raft got in the way. We decided then that it would be much better if this equipment were all hooked to a single length of rope and that one rope fastened to the side of the raft. The Jap evidently did not spot us because he continued directly on his course. Later on the same day we saw some P-38s at about 7,000 or 8,000 feet. We put out the chemical sea marker which we had; and it worked very well, making a large bright green splotch on the water all around the raft; however, the P-38s continued on their course without seeing us. About dusk another plane came over, and at first we thought it was a C-47. We were about to fire our flare pistol when our pilot decided not to since there was no visible escort for the C-47, and it was unlikely that one of our ships would be flying alone in this area. As soon as it got closer we could see that it was a Jap DC-2. Once more we had to get out of the raft and turned it over, and once more the Jap failed to spot us. About one and a half hours later some low-flying P-40s came directly over our position. We attempted to use the signaling flashlight, but it failed to operate so we grabbed the flare pistol. It was the type of flare pistol that has to hit on the base with the palm of your hand in order to fire, but this too failed to work. We all thought that the cause of this failure on the part of these two pieces of equipment was water, since they were both pretty well soaked. Had they been contained in some waterproof material, there is no doubt in our minds but that we could have signaled these P-40s since they were flying directly over our raft and were at a minimum altitude.

At about 11:00 the second night, we decided that we were going ashore on an island which we had spotted. We did not know exactly where we were but figured that since there had been no apparent drifting, we should still be somewhere in the vicinity of Leyte. We went ashore and filled our cans with water and were talking over our situation when we saw some lights coming down the shore. They looked as though they were flashlights; and since we didn't know whether they were Japs or Filipino guerrillas, we got back into the raft and paddled off-shore about one-half mile or so.

By 10:00 of the next morning we were about two miles off shore, and we sighted an outrigger about a mile further out. We paddled up to it and saw that it apparently contained a native fisherman; but since it was difficult to tell who was and who wasn't friendly to our forces in this area, we advanced with extreme caution. He appeared to be quite friendly; but nevertheless, as soon as we pulled up alongside his outrigger, two of us grabbed him while the third checked the outrigger and fisherman for weapons of any kind or for papers that would indicate where his sympathies lay. We were unable to converse with him since he knew no English, but managed to make our requests for food and water understood by sign language. Using sign language himself, he indicated that he would give us food and water if we would follow him into shore. Since the Japs are offering very high rewards for American airmen downed in this area, our pilot feared a trap, so he told us to stay in the raft and remain hidden while he went in with the native in the outrigger. If everything was okay he was to signal us to come ashore. About an hour later we saw the lieutenant standing on the beach waving to us to come in. The Filipino provided us with food, water, and shelter and dispatched a native runner to 32nd Division Headquarters. Four days later an Alligator arrived at the camp and took us to headquarters.

From our experience I would say that the most important thing to remember when ditching in aircraft is to keep your head, do things as you have been instructed to do them in ditching practice, and keep your equipment as dry as possible. I would also suggest that the equipment of the rafts be checked more often by ground maintenance in the group and that those pieces of equipment which are not already in absolutely watertight containers be waterproofed.

Also, the importance of efficient ditching practice and good air discipline cannot be overemphasized. In our case lack of this air discipline on the part of two men cost them their lives. They undoubtedly felt that traveling at the high speed we were with our gear down, we would all be killed when we hit anyway. As it turned out, the only man who was killed was riding aft of the pilot at the spot where the ship broke in two; and the men who jumped from the waist would, if they had stayed in their positions, have undoubtedly survived the landing.

23

A Ship in the Night

LT. (JG) R. B. Plaister, USN

The course of our attack is described in the ACA report to which this statement is appended.

After turning hard to port and closing my bomb bay doors, I applied as much power as possible, trying to make continuous, gradual turns and changes in altitude, as the A/A was accurate and intense. Just after I commenced jinking, I remember hearing the crewmen conversing about the odor of something burning. A shell had just exploded very near, but at first I didn't notice any evidence of damage to the plane.

Then about 30 seconds later, my gunner, Smith, called and said that the plane was afire and smoking badly. I tried to call but my ICS was out. I then looked out of the cockpit and observed considerable hot oil on the starboard stub wing. I observed also that my plane had lost all oil pressure. My first thought was for all of us to bail out, but this thought was discarded when I saw we had only about 500 feet altitude. I did this because I believed it safer to make a water landing with speed acquired by pushing over from 500 feet than to risk a power landing with an engine which I expected to freeze any moment. Thus, I nosed over, built up speed, and pulled out with sufficient speed to pop my flaps and made a fairly good landing. Fortunately I was headed into the wind at the time. Before hitting the water, I checked my straps and braced myself for the splash. When in the water, I got out on a wing as quickly as possible but, from having my face jammed into the gun sight, was stunned. Smith called that he had the big life raft out. Then, as I started to get my seat raft open, I slipped off into the water. Being hazy, I hadn't inflated my life jacket. I was pulled down a great deal by my heavy shoes and chute. I finally got to the big raft, with the help of an oar which Smith held out. With his help I then inflated my life jacket and the small (one man) life raft.

Smith, meantime, had been instrumental in getting my radioman, Tomes, out of the radio compartment thru the turret, as Tomes had been dazed by smoke and the landing. Smith finally got Tomes in the raft. Tomes believes his belt broke, as he sustained a deep gash in his head, which bled quite profusely. He had opened the door believing he might jump.

Once in the life rafts which we lashed together, we broke out the first aid kits. We applied sulfanilamide to Tomes' head and applied a bandage. We also applied the same drug to my nose and lip, which was later sewed up after we were picked up. Although we felt pretty good about the prospect of being rescued we nevertheless went about preparing things in the event we had to make our own way.

First, we took stock of things aboard; we found the following:

An inflation pump, ten (10) cans of water

Two first aid kits, repair equipment for rafts

3 cans of meat, sealed up rations

3 Ponchos, oars in 2 man raft

Fishing kits, hand paddles in one man raft

Very pistol and shells, two bailing cups

2 compasses, 2 flash lights

Lashing our equipment and supplies securely, we studied our wind and current and figured our possible drift and best place to head, and decided we would head for Luzon if we weren't picked up.

About 1500, we noticed a Jap cruiser hovering about near the horizon at about five or six miles to the southwest. We rowed east for a while to get as far away as possible. Soon he changed course, so we stopped rowing. He finally disappeared to the south. He did open with A/A at times, but we saw no planes.

At about 1630 we spied another cruiser (Kuma, with three bulbous stacks) to the south and again we started rowing east. This cruiser passed at about three miles to the west of us heading north. He was followed by a destroyer that came close and we stopped rowing and covered the rafts with blue ponchos. This destroyer changed his course and came directly towards us until he was about 400 yards away. He then turned and headed north, thank God! A few minutes later we heard and later saw planes which attacked this cruiser and destroyer and a battle ship whose superstructure we could see on the horizon. We couldn't see the results of their attack.

At sunset we took a little water and prepared for the night by covering ourselves with ponchos. Every once in a while water would come in the rafts, and we'd have to bail.

At approximately 1930 some firing started from south of us, shells passing over us en route north and then return fire from the Jap north of us. The firing became very intense from the southward; the firing from the north eased off. Under any other circumstances, this sight would have been very interesting. On hearing the guns to the south I hoped it was from our battleships but it proved to be our cruisers. They hit one Jap ship, as there was a tremendous flash and explosion to the north. However, our ships to the south kept firing for over half an hour. By this time there was hardly any return fire.

Not very much later, three of our destroyers headed north passed very close to us, and we flashed a flash light at them. We were later told that an observer on one destroyer had spotted the light but thought it might be a reflection from the moon. Things then became quiet, and our hopes dropped as the destroyers passed out of sight to the north.

At about 2200 I thought I heard something and looked around and saw a ship approaching us from the north. I believed it must be one of our ships and woke the men and they flashed a light. The destroyer closed and half circled us and called. About that time, Smith managed to fire a star shell with the Very pistol. The shell was not projected from the pistol, but did burn in the barrel, which Smith held. After quite a few calls the destroyer recognized our yell of "San Jacinto" and told us to come close to the ship under the bridge. We were picked up at about 2230.

GLOSSARY OF TERMS USED IN THE BOOK

U.S. NAVY AIRPLANES

U.S. Navy aircraft and squadron nomenclature. Each squadron has an alphanumeric designator such as VF-26. "V" means fixed wing aviation, the etymology of which is unclear, while "F" indicates the squadron's mission. VF is a fighter squadron; VF-26 would be fighter squadron number 26.

VF - Navy fighter squadron

VB - Navy bombing squadron

VG - escort-scouting squadron

VP - Navy patrol squadron

VC - Navy scouting squadron

VT - Navy torpedo squadron

VP - Navy seaplane patrol squadron

VPB - Navy seaplane patrol bombing squadron

VPH - patrol squadron (heavy)

VOS - Navy observation or scout squadron

P - patrol or scout plane

VM - the addition of an "M" signifies a Marine squadron, as in VMF or VMB

F4U - Corsair, a single-seat fighter

F4F - Wildcat, a single-seat fighter

F6F - Hellcat, a carrier-based single-seat fighter

OS2U - Kingfisher, a single-engine floatplane; usually carried by a battleship

PBY - Catalina, a large twin-engine seaplane; used in rescue and combat

PB4Y - large four-engine patrol bomber; a Navy version of the B-24

PBM - Mariner, a large twin-engine seaplane; used in rescue and combat

SB2C - carrier-based two-man dive or torpedo bomber

TBF/TBM - three-man dive or torpedo bomber

U.S. NAVY SHIPS

CV - aircraft carrier

CVE - escort carrier; smaller than a CV

DD - first line Navy destroyer

DE - destroyer escort; also a tin can

LCI - landing ship infantry; carried about 200 soldiers

U.S. AIR FORCE PLANES

A-20 - Havoc, a medium twin-engine bomber

B-17 - Fortress, a mainstay four-engine heavy bomber

B-24 - Liberator, a mainstay four-engine heavy bomber

B-25 - Mitchell, a twin-engine medium bomber

B-29 - Superfortress, a heavy four-engine pressurized bomber; used to bomb Japan

P-38 - Lightning, a twin-engine frontline fighter

P-47 - Thunderbolt, a single-engine frontline fighter

L-5 - Sentinel, a single-engine spotter plane; looks like today's Cessna 180s

C-47 - military version of the civilian DC-3; used as a troop carrier

BRITISH PLANES

Spitfire - single-seat fighter

Hudson - twin-engine light attack bomber; built by Lockheed for the British Coastal Command

GERMAN PLANES

FW-190 - single-seat Luftwaffe fighter

RESCUE GEAR

MF DF or MF/DF - British medium frequency direction finding wireless station; used to pinpoint location on downed aircraft

bolo knife - traditional Filipino knife with a long, curving blade

Carlisle first aid packet - small tin carried by soldiers named after the Carlisle Barracks, where the Army developed medical equipment and field dressings; contained gauze and sulfanilamide

Mae West - life vest that draped around the neck; when inflated, it looked like the bosoms of the actress Mae West

Very gun/flare - stub-nosed flare gun developed by Edward Very

Lindholme rescue gear - 300-foot-long length of rope to which four buoyant cylinders were attached, one of which had rafts, food, guns, etc.; the idea was to drape the rope near a downed aircrew so they could pull the rest in

Airborne lifeboat - rigid canoe-like lifeboat affixed to the belly of a B-17 and parachuted down to a downed crew

E-3 kit - small personal survival kit containing matches, malted milk balls, halazone tablets, a compass, and such

Gibson Girl - hour-glass-shaped hand-cranked radio that broadcast in Morse Code; named after the fashion artist Charles Gibson, who was known for his narrow-waisted models

IFF - identification friend or foe transponders that broadcast a confirming code

LOST USAGE:

syrettes/styrettes - single-dose glass ampoules with needles and medicines, usually morphine

halazone tablet - water purification tablet

JAPANESE PLANES

Betty - twin-engine land-based bomber

Frances - twin-engine land-based bomber

Jack - somewhat dated Mitsubishi single-seat fighter

Kate - single-engine carrier-based bomber

Oscar - single-engine land-based fighter

Pete - single-engine floatplane; like our Kingfisher

Sally - twin-engine land-based bomber

Tony - single-engine land-based fighter

Val - single-engine carrier-based dive bomber

Zeke - single-engine carrier-based fighter

Zero - single-engine carrier-based fighter

ABBREVIATIONS AND NICKNAMES NOT OTHERWISE EXPLAINED

AA/AAA - anti-aircraft fire/anti-aircraft artillery

ACI - Air Combat Intelligence, the combat intelligence section that briefed pilots on Navy ships

a/f - airfield

ASR - air-sea rescue

Black Cat - PBY Catalina designed to operate at night

can/tin can - small Navy ship called a DE, or destroyer escort, which, because of its small size, was called a "tin can" or a "can"

Dumbo - PBY Catalina, PBM Mariner, or any large flying boat rescue aircraft

e/a - enemy aircraft

Hood - now called the canopy; the clear enclosure over the cockpit of a fighter plane

RAF - Royal Air Force (England)

RAAF - Royal Australian Air Force

USFFE - United States Forces Far East

INDEX

ABOUT THE AUTHOR

L. Douglas Keeney is the author of more than a dozen histories on the events that shaped the American landscape including his bestseller on the *Cold War 15 Minutes: General Curtis LeMay and the Countdown to Nuclear Annihilation* and his definitive study of Earth photography in *Lights of Mankind: Earth at Night As Seen from Space*. Including his two previous titles, *This is Guadalcanal* and *Air War Pacific*, this is his third book on the Pacific Theater of World War II. Mr. Keeney holds a Masters degree from the University of Southern California, is a skilled pilot, and is the editor of the *Lost Histories of World War II* series.

www.douglaskeeney.com